Receive Yo

MICHAEL HANSEN S. J.

Receive Your Healing

Meditations for the road to recovery

Marshall Pickering
An Imprint of HarperCollins*Publishers*

Marshall Pickering is an Imprint of
HarperCollins*Religious*
Part of HarperCollins*Publishers*
77–85 Fulham Palace Road,
Hammersmith, London W6 8JB

First published in Australia in 1993 by Collins Dove as
The Land of Walking Trees
First published in Great Britain
in 1994 by Marshall Pickering
1 3 5 7 9 8 6 4 2

Michael Hansen asserts the moral right to
be identified as the author of this work

A catalogue record for this book is
available from the British Library

ISBN 0 551 02816 5

Set in Garamond

Printed in Great Britain by
HarperCollinsManufacturing Glasgow

DEDICATED
to the memory of my father, Lel Hansen

to my mother, Berna Hansen,
and my family who have supported and prayed for me:
Chris and Judy, Robert and Michele, Nicholas and
Frances, John and Kate, Mary and Neil, Bernadette and
Alan, Patrick, Sean and Cheryl, Jeanne and my
twenty-three nieces and nephews

to my relatives and friends
who have travelled with me on this journey:
Margaret, Jim and Betty, Bob, Ruth, Val, Ian and
Wendy, Peggy and Brian, Rosemary and Paul, Doug
and Mary

to my Jesuit brothers,
especially the communities of St Mary's Parish and
Canisius College. To my close Jesuit friends who have
shown me again and again the graces to be found in
this time of my life

to my doctors and counsellor,
Brian, Tim, Terry and Ron

to the ME/CFS Society of NSW
whose support I have found invaluable

to Saint Ignatius of Loyola,
who suffered chronic illness and whose vision included
the insight that we can discover the purpose and
meaning of our lives in both health and illness.

CONTENTS

ACKNOWLEDGEMENTS

*My thanks to Fr Brendan Kelly SJ
for his insights and help in preparing
the manuscript.*

INTRODUCTION

Jesus came to Bethsaida. Some people brought a blind man to him and begged him to touch him. He took the blind man by the hand and led him out of the village; and when he had put saliva on his eyes and laid hands on him, he asked him, 'Can you see anything?' And the man looked up and said, 'I can see people, but they look like trees, walking.' Then Jesus laid his hands on his eyes again; and he looked intently and his sight was restored, and he saw everything clearly.

Mark 8:22–25

Why is the blind man not healed at first touch? Is the healing power of Jesus beginning to fail? Or does this unusual story point to something deeper about healing? Anyone with chronic illness would love to be instantly healed. But the reality is that we live in a half-world where we are neither totally incapacitated nor totally healthy. This unusual healing story speaks to us in a special way.

Imagine, like the blind man, you have been living in a land of darkness. At last you have the chance to see. Your friends take you to the healer and you feel his hand in yours. He takes you outside the village and away from your familiar surroundings. At the very least you would feel both hope and fear.

Imagine the healer stops you. You wonder what is happening. You feel a wetness on your eyes. Your eyes clear and you see a land where people look like walking trees. You are half-sighted and half-blind! At the very least you would feel both hope and anxiety.

Imagine you hear the healer ask 'Can you see anything?' You strain to see but the world around you is indistinct. The healing is a failure. At the very least you would feel disappointment and anger.

These feelings of darkness and anxiety, of hope and fear, of disappointment and anger are no stranger to those of us with chronic illness. We seem to live in a half-way place—a land of walking trees.

In the last two years I have had myalgic encephalomyelitis or chronic fatigue syndrome (CFS). I have been unable to work and, at times, been unable to do very little of anything. The meditations in this book chart the landmarks of my journey in the land of walking trees. It is, of course, a journey I am still making—what follows in this book is a diary of hopes and not final resolutions.

As I write this introduction I am neither the best I have been nor the worst. I wish I could say all my prayers have been answered but all I can say is that healing has come in places I never expected. One thing I have come to believe is that our faith is more about openness of heart to take the journey, to keep moving forward, than it is about reaching any imagined destination.

All the texts in this book have been taken from the gospel of Luke—the testimony of a man who was a doctor by profession. Luke arranged his gospel in such a way that Jesus appears to take one long journey from Nazareth to Jerusalem—from birth to death and resurrection. It is a traveller's gospel. It is a pilgrim's guide. It speaks in a special way to those of us who suddenly find we are on a journey that we never expected, and one that we were never prepared for.

In reading the stories of others with CFS I have often seen descriptions of this journey. It has two sides. The outer journey of the physical course of the illness and the inner journey of the spirit. Some speak of 'having to clean out the cupboards', others of discovering 'new strengths'. Whatever the language, chronic illness takes us on an inner journey into new territory. This can be a profoundly unsettling experience.

Most sufferers of CFS can look forward to full recovery. Many other chronic illnesses take one on a journey of slow deterioration or leave one on a permanent level of self-limitation. Common to all, however, is the experience of living with a chronic disability over many years. We live it daily and it changes us and those who are close to us. So where is the hope in all of this?

In every healing story in the gospels the one element necessary is faith. Where there is no faith, Jesus cannot heal. Each healing story is an invitation to faith. Miracles are just like the reality of chronic illness. They have an outer and an inner story to tell. The action of the healing miracle always points to a deeper reality. It is wise to note that expecting signs and miracles often renders Jesus impotent. So what is this deeper reality?

It is that Jesus offers life. He offers new life in the face of disease, hunger, poverty and death. One can live fully whatever the physical situation, including death itself. Our dignity, uniqueness and lovableness do not depend on our performance or our limitation. We are offered life right where we are now. This is the cause of our hope. In every sense the end of the blind man's story can be the end of our story.

Imagine the touch of the healer a second time. He puts his hands on your eyes. As he removes his hands the world around you sharpens. You can see clearly and distinctly. You are healed. At the very least, you would be filled with wonder and joy.

How to use this book

This book is intended to be dipped into rather than to be read cover to cover. All the meditations use the gospel text and imagination in a prayer method taught by St Ignatius. The aim of this book is simply to bring oneself into relationship with God.

In your prayer choose the image of God that you feel most comfortable with. Throughout this book I speak of the Lord, but you could equally pray with the Spirit, God the Father, God the Mother, or with any other image of God. With this in mind, here are three ways to use this book.

The first way is to choose one of the meditations. Read it slowly. Read it again, and this time be aware of any phrase or image that evokes feelings or resonates with your own experience. Stop at the words or image that move you. This is where the spirit is prompting you. Do not worry about the rest. Put the book down and ask the Lord to come into your presence. Then sit with the image or the words. Stay there. In following days return to the same image or words. In time you will know when to move on.

The second way is read the meditations and note which ones you find yourself returning to. Choose one of these. Read the scripture text. Put the book down and use all of your senses to imagine the scene in the text. Imagine the place, the setting, the details of the scene. Imagine the people, what they look like, what they are doing. Hear the words spoken. Place yourself in the scene. Take the place of the person you most identify with. Feel, taste, see, hear and touch what that person experiences. Meet the Lord in the scene. Let your feelings, experience and imagination lead you. Listen to the Lord. Imagine the Lord's response. Make your own response.

The third way is to note which meditations seem closest to your own experience or your own desires. Choose one. Take a section and use it as a bridge to recapture your own experience. Go back in your imagination to the strongest memory of that experience. Relive it in the presence of the Lord. Imagine the Lord listening. Imagine the Lord with you in that experience. Stand, as it were, beside the Lord as the scene replays itself. Imagine the Lord's response to the events and people in the scene. Imagine the Lord's response to you. Express your feelings to the Lord. Ask the Lord for healing of your memory, of yourself now. In this, you have returned to the present and can finish with a short prayer of thanks for the way the Lord encounters you in your life.

Once you feel comfortable with any of these methods you will be ready to pray the gospels yourself. As with all prayer books, this is the time to put aside the book and meet the Lord in your own experience.

PROLOGUE

For this reason I bow my knees before the Father, from whom every family in heaven and on earth takes its name.

I pray that, according to the riches of his glory, he may grant that you may be strengthened in your inner being with power through his spirit, and that Christ may dwell in your hearts through faith, as you are being rooted and grounded in love.

I pray that you may have the power to comprehend, with all the saints, what is the breadth and length and height and depth, and to know the love of Christ that surpasses knowledge, so that you may be filled with all the fullness of God.

Now to him who by the power at work within us is able to accomplish abundantly far more than all we could ask or imagine, to him be glory in the church and in Christ Jesus to all generations, forever and ever. Amen.

Ephesians 3:14–21

Barrenness
Luke 1:36–37

The Angel Gabriel said to Mary, 'And now, your relative Elizabeth in her old age has also conceived a son; and this is the sixth month for her who was said to be barren. For nothing will be impossible with God.'

SAID TO BE BARREN

Nothing will be impossible with God

The Pilgrim

Lord, I remember vividly the day the doctor told me I had a chronic illness. My feelings were like chained dogs suddenly let free. Relief bolted first. I was not going crazy. It was not in my mind. I had a real disease and it had a name. Elation followed relief. All the confusion, the deep down anxiety, the years of pushing on were over. I had a disease. I told the doctor it was wonderful news.

Then came the grieving, the dark dreams, the sense of loss and emptiness. This illness was not going to be over in a few days, or next week, or even next year. I was not going to be able to take a little break and return to normal life. What was I to do? What would my friends think? How would I cope?

As the disease took hold of me I found even the smallest things were beyond me. Then, one night, panic paid a noisy visit and sent all my other feelings running for cover. It stayed for weeks. It paralysed me. Finally, having had its way, panic left me in the hands of barrenness.

Lord, I feel so useless and empty. Is there anything more useless than one who is chronically ill? I am unproductive. I am unfruitful. I am barren of energy, action, movement—even the will to see things differently. What is left when a disease takes so much from one? I cannot call myself a provider, a helper, or a worker. It is so hard to drop the labels. I cannot call myself a nurturer, a listener or a supporter. I do not have the energy. What can I call myself?

I am confused, Lord. All the roles in my family have changed. Yet I do not want to change and neither do they. I am a husk, an empty thing, a barren life. Lord, I pray for acceptance. I am chronically ill and I can change nothing. It is impossible for my life to be otherwise. Help me to accept this.

The Lord

Why should I? Nothing will be impossible with God. The Lord God created life from emptiness. What makes you think our Creator would abandon you now? Know this: I am the God of the living not the dead. I am the Lord of life. I have walked the same path of helplessness. In Gethsemane I cried out in panic. On a cross I died helpless and powerless. I know your panic and your grief. I too was stripped of everything. My life was a seed that had to die. So is yours.

I created you. In you is the seed of life and fruitfulness. Who told you that such life rested in your ability to perform? Who told you your fruitfulness came from being a provider, a helper, a listener or any other label you cling to so hard?

I love you. You are much more than any of these labels. Drop them. Your dignity is always within you. Drop them and relish what is left— yourself.

In the end you are fragile, weak, confused, but not useless. I did not create you barren. As you let go of the labels, you will begin to come into the true fruitfulness of your being. I will grace your life a hundredfold. Our Creator is nothing but extravagant. He is a God of surprises and you are already pregnant with new life. Your illness will give birth to many new possibilities. Nothing will be impossible with God.

I promise you this much. I will be with you for the term. I will breathe with you. I will rub your back during the pain of giving birth. I will celebrate when you hold the fragile, new-born child. I will be gladdened as you draw this part of yourself close to your heart.

Rejoice! You who people call barren are with child.

Prayer

Lord help me to let go of all the labels in my life. I cannot be the performer I was before. I cannot be the provider, the worker, the helper I was before. You are leading me to a new freedom. Help me to cherish this freedom, a freedom so painfully won.

Thank you for the new possibilities of my life. I do not know what I shall give birth to. I do know I have a new life growing within me. Help me to be patient. Help me to let go of the past and rest peacefully in the present.

I cannot offer you anything other than my presence and my prayer. Do not abandon me now. I know you will not do so, but in the dark times I need you to remind me of your love.

I do not know how I will be tomorrow or next week. I cannot plan for the future, but I can live fully now and by your grace keep hoping. I can be certain that this illness is revealing the true wonder of my being.

I am afraid of dying within myself and yet I

ponder what shall be born anew. Nothing will be impossible with you. Tell me again, Lord, that I am not barren. Tell me again.

Poverty
Luke 2:1–12

In those days a decree went out from Emperor Augustus that the whole world should be registered. This was the first registration and was taken when Quirinius was governor of Syria. All went to their own towns to be registered. Joseph also went from the town of Nazareth in Galilee to Judea, to the city of David called Bethlehem, because he was descended from the house and family of David. He went to be registered with Mary, to whom he was engaged and who was expecting a child.

While they were there, the time came for her to deliver her child. And she gave birth to her first-born son and wrapped him in bands of cloth, and laid him in a manger, because there was no place for them in the inn.

In that region there were shepherds living in the fields, keeping watch over their flock by night. Then an angel of the Lord stood before them, and the glory of the Lord shone around them, and they were terrified. But the angel said to them, 'Do not be afraid; For see—I am bringing you good news of great joy for all the people: to you is born this day in the city of David a Saviour, who is the Messiah, the Lord. This will be a sign for you: you will find a baby wrapped in bands of cloth and lying in a manger.'

LAID IN A MANGER
Wrapped in bands of cloth

The Pilgrim

Lord, I have travelled far in this illness. I had no choice. My illness has taken control. I never anticipated this inner journey.

I have looked at my past life. All the old hurts and angers have to go. They are burdens I can no longer carry.

I have journeyed into the territory of my desires and fears. I have come home to myself. For the most part it has been a lonely and painful road. It is all quite different from what I expected. I always thought I knew myself, but I am home and I feel homeless. I am a refugee unto myself.

I find myself in a crude shelter, a place held together by faith and hope. It is a drafty place. Cold winds of fear and doubt find their way through the walls. It is a place where the beasts of my unconscious are stabled. Some I fear, some have surprised me, some have revealed strengths I never knew I had. We are all restless. We are all stabled together.

I have journeyed home and discovered my fragility and poverty. Anxiety and expectation shoulder each other. They stamp their feet. I can feel their warm breath on my neck. Things that seemed precious to me have become soiled and downtrodden—dirty straw on the floor of my shelter.

And yet I feel strangely at home. Something is comforting in this stable. Tools of planting and harvesting lie about me; a sack of seeds for next season's planting, a hoe for weeding and a scythe for reaping. Behind me are beasts to help in the harvest.

I am frightened by my poverty and yet I know, perhaps for the first time in many years, that this is a true part of me, my deepest self. What am I to make of this journey, this place, this poverty? My Lord, what have you planned for this night?

The Lord

Rest where you are now. Let go. This night you are a new-born child. Naked and needy you have nothing, and yet in this poverty you have everything.

Rest with me as I was, a child in a manger. Rest where you are now so I can gaze on you in love. In my eyes you are the most precious child on earth. You are mine. I will wrap you in bands of cloth. I will feed you and care for you. Could I forget you now? Everything about you is a delight for me. The more so because you are so helpless, so new born that I can do nothing else but hold you close.

When I see you in your poverty my heart fills with a deep joy, for this is your hidden self, your true self, and I know you will grow strong.

Now you are so vulnerable, so precious, so special. When I see you like this every cell in my being cries out to care for you and to shield you from all harm.

Rest where you are and let me tend to your

needs. You do not have to win me over. I am yours already. Do nothing. Relish the manger. Snuggle down in your bands of cloth. With me at your side you will never be richer or stronger or more fully yourself.

Do not be afraid. Your hand is small in mine. I will not let you go. I have eyes only for you. My love is fierce and proud.

To find you as you are now makes me want to change the course of the stars. I want to let the whole world know how special you are. Let your friends bring gifts. Let the poor see your poverty. Let your God wonder at the marvel of your being. Let the angels sing and all creation rejoice at your birth.

On this night rest where you are. Rest in your poverty. Let us welcome you home.

Prayer

You astonish me, Lord. If you had asked me to climb a mountain, I would have done it. I would have gone anywhere to free myself from the helplessness of this illness.

If you had asked me to do certain deeds in the future I would have sworn an oath. I would have done anything to escape the shame, the confusion and the helplessness of my poverty.

Yet you bid me to rest where I am. You ask me to rest in my poverty. You delight in me as I am now.

Help me to let go into your hands. Let me bask in your love. You have shown me how I can rest safe in the arms of your fierce and tender love. Let me rest my small hands in yours.

I am amazed that you care for me so much—especially now. You speak of the delight you find in me. Tell me again, Lord. It will take a long time for me to find the same relish in my weakness and poverty. I am dumbfounded with the excess of your love. In my illness teach me how to receive your love and the love of my family and friends.

In this crude shelter of my birth show me where to find the seeds for planting in the next harvest—the harvest of my life to come.

Paralysis
Luke 5:17–26

One day, while Jesus was teaching, Pharisees and teachers of the law were sitting near by (they had come from every village of Galilee and Judea and from Jerusalem); and the power of the Lord was with him to heal. Just then some men came, carrying a paralysed man on a bed. They were trying to bring him in and lay him before Jesus; but finding no way to bring him in because of the crowd, they climbed up on the roof and let him down with his bed through the tiles into the middle of the crowd in front of Jesus.

When he saw their faith, he said, 'Friend, your sins are forgiven you.' Then the scribes and the Pharisees began to question, 'Who is this who is speaking blasphemies? Who can forgive sins but God alone?' When Jesus perceived their questioning, he answered them, 'Why do you raise such questions in your hearts? Which is easier, to say, "Your sins are forgiven you", or to say, "Stand up and walk"?'

'But so that you may know that the Son of

Man has authority on earth to forgive sins'—
he said to the one who was paralysed—'I say
to you, "Stand up and take your bed and go
to your home".'

Immediately he stood up before them, took
what he had been lying on, and went to his
home, glorifying God. Amazement seized all of
them, they glorified God and were filled with
awe, saying, 'We have seen strange things to-
day!'

CARRIED BY FRIENDS

Stand up and walk

The Pilgrim

How well I know this bed, my Lord. This chair, this room, this small world that is now mine. Every crack and mark in the ceiling has been traced a hundred times by the finger of my mind. I have watched a spider build a web in the corner. I saw its beginning, the thin regular tracery of its making and I saw its ending. Now it's just one long dirty strand twisting in the air above my bed. Each piece of furniture in my room has become an old friend—each piece now stands mute about me in a wooden vigil.

My small world has nothing left to offer me. I've moved the items on my desk and arranged the covers on the bed and still the day stretches before me. Who would have thought I'd make so much of morning tea? Even my friend's visits seem tasteless. My own family have become like missionaries from a faraway land.

As I look down over my body, the memories

of running, carrying, lifting and swimming all flood through me—phantom limbs on a phantom body. I feel paralysed. My body can do so very little and my mind can remember so much.

I cannot accept I am sick in this way. I cannot go back to where I was—my body won't take me there. I cannot go forward. This half-way place, this barren place of the spirit has paralysed me. My hard won life's wisdom is useless.

I do not know what to do. I have no more prayers, no more words. My mind is black frustration. My body is stretched and stretchered.

The Lord

Do not be afraid. Open your eyes. I tell you the small world you live in is as wide as the universe. I have placed the whole of my loving design into the smallest flower, into the curve of every wood grain, into the rushed visit of every friend who does not know what to say. Do you know that the single touch of a friend or a lover or a stranger holds in it the same touch that created the world and every living thing? Open your eyes!

You now live to a more powerful time, to a deeper changing, to a more fertile growing. See the gift I have given you in nature's time. You no longer have to live to the rush of the second hand, or to the tyranny of the hour hand barking out the next duty.

You, my precious one, have been given the gift of season's time. You can live apace and apeace with winter's long promise and springs slow flowering. You are the bare branch and the seed and the flower. Rejoice! Rejoice where you are right now!

Pick up your stretcher. Listen to me. You can walk from this half-way place. You are hurting because you are at last discovering your true worth.

I have special gifts for you. Listen to the slow heartbeat of your own spirit. It walks gently into its own springtime. Come home to yourself! The best of yourself awaits you. Return to the vast wonder of your small world—you have the legs for it and this is enough.

Give thanks for your friends. They carried you and lowered you before me with their love and prayers, even when you did not know it. Share in their lives without jealousy. Who knows? Perhaps their world is smaller than yours. Perhaps someone is waiting for you to rip the roof off their prison and free them from their paralysis.

Prayer

Lord of life I thank you for opening my eyes to the wonder of my small world. Help me to rest here and see anew the whole of creation. Let me see the vibrant tracery of life in the flowers by my bed. Let me see the exuberant designs of nature in the trees outside my window. Let me see the playful touch of your hand in the smallest things.

Thank you for the gift of season's time. My anxiety falls away when I relax into winter's promise. Tension unfolds as I begin to sense the slow enlivening of spring. Summer heralds a dance of warmth and life. Autumn calls for the quiet, inevitable shedding of old cares.

Thank you for the gift of my friends. I pray for them and their needs. Please send your healing and enlivening spirit to each of them. Help me to learn from their faith.

Lord of new life I am in your hands. Let me feel their creative touch, their subtleness, their gentleness and their strength of purpose. Open my eyes to the sheer extravagance of your creativity.

Lord of the living I look forward to the deepening of my own freedom. As I find it, may I help any others who find themselves paralysed.

Power

Luke 4:1–13

Jesus, full of the Holy Spirit, returned from the Jordan and was led by the Spirit in the wilderness, where for forty days he was tempted by the devil. He ate nothing at all during those days, and when they were over, he was famished. The devil said to him, 'If you are the Son of God, command this stone to become a loaf of bread.' Jesus answered him, 'It is written, "One does not live by bread alone".'

Then the devil led him up and showed him in an instant all the kingdoms of the world. And the devil said to him, 'To you I will give their glory and all this authority; for it has been given over to me, and I give it to anyone I please. If you, then, will worship me, it will all be yours.' Jesus answered him, 'It is written, "Worship the Lord your God, and serve only him".'

Then the devil took him to Jerusalem, and placed him on the pinnacle of the temple, saying to him, 'If you are the Son of God, throw yourself down from here, for it is written, "He will command his angels concerning you, to *protect you," and "On their hands they will bear you up, so that you will not dash your foot against a stone".'*

Jesus answered him, 'It is said, "Do not put the Lord your God to the test".' When the devil had finished every test, he departed from him until an opportune time.

IN THE WILDERNESS
Led by the Spirit

The Pilgrim

This illness has led me into a wilderness. The familiar landmarks of my life are gone. Worse, there are no distractions here—just hard stones and voices. 'You are useless now,' taunts the voice of old strengths. 'You could do this before . . . people respected you then . . . remember how good you felt.' I push against my illness. I relapse, and somewhere inside, the strong one holds on and bides time. It whispers, 'Never let go that which makes you who you are—your strength and powers.'

This illness has led me into a wasteland. The voice of old glories mocks me, 'You are worthless now.' It takes me to a place high over the kingdom I have built around myself. 'Look at what you have achieved, look at the place you have won for yourself before others.' Afterwards I get angry. My friends seem to have forgotten what I have achieved. I tell them that I am still the same, but my illness drags me back into the wasteland. Deep inside I throw another wall around my kingdom. 'Never let them take this from you, a voice whispers, 'your successes measure your worth.'

This illness has led me into a desert. I am not alone. Friends and family, doctors and supporters surround me. 'You have to depend on others,' scorns the voice of my old independence. 'Rely on no one,' it whispers, 'this illness is just another challenge. You will beat it all by yourself. Besides, you do not want to put anyone out, do you?' These words fill me up. I brush aside help. I find myself alone in the desert. 'A small set-back,' whispers my pride, 'remember you control your own life.'

This illness has led me to a barren place. I hunger for my old self, my old life. I feed on my old strengths and powers, my past glories and independence. They make me who I am. So, tell me Lord, why am I still famished?

The Lord

You are hungry because half-truths make a poor meal for the desert dweller. I know. I was there myself. I was led into the wilderness and tempted by the voices of our humanity. They are a part of us that will always strain towards power, strength and independence. We all want to feel we are in control.

The half-truth is that these things are not evil in themselves. But it is a subtle voice that seeks to take you from where you are now—in the wilderness with nothing; hungry, weak, vulnerable and needy. This is the other side of our humanity.

In the desert there are no distractions. Your illness helps you to see clearly. Your vulnerability is a light shining deep within your inner self. You can see the kingdoms you have built around yourself. The voices of your false self tell you to build another wall. I tell you, unless you let those walls fall you will be imprisoned by them forever. Let your hidden self out. I have long loved what I saw there deep within you. Others will too.

You do not have all your old strengths. They may return in time, they may not. It does not matter. You will learn a new strength, one that will never fail you—the strength of rejoicing in yourself just as you are. Neither strengths nor weaknesses make you who you are. You are you. Go gladly with your humanity. You do not need control.

I found it difficult too. I was offered the chance to do what I came for—to feed the hungry and to draw all the kingdoms to myself. My voices knew all my desires. How hard it is to let go of power! How hard it is to trust in the weakness of our humanity and the strength of our God. There are no certainties on this road, only that I have gone before you.

All life in the desert has to play a waiting game. Be patient. The seeds of your hidden self will germinate under the barrenness of the desert soil.

Prayer

Lord, take and receive my strength and my weakness, my independence and my trust, my achievements and my powerlessness. Help me to accept all of my humanity.

Open my ears to hear the voices in the desert. Only then can I bring them to light. Only then can I see them for what they are—temptations to run away from the reality of my humanity, the reality of where this illness has led me.

Lord, it is hard to hand over power and control. My illness shows me how much I need you, how much I need the love and care of my family and friends. I am frightened by what I see in myself.

May the vulnerability I feel be a gentle light that shows me the way to my true self. May the powerlessness I feel place me in the hands of the Creator. Be company to me as my hidden self grows strong.

One special grace I ask. I would like to share my experience of the desert with those who love me. It is a precious part of myself now. Help me to do this gently, when the time is right.

Give me the courage and the faith to let fall the walls of the kingdom I have built around myself.

Give me the patience to wait for the flowers in the desert of my illness.

Anger
Luke 4:16–30

When Jesus came to Nazareth, where he had
been brought up, he went to the synagogue on
the Sabbath day, as was his custom. He stood
up to read, and the scroll of the prophet
Isaiah was given to him. He unrolled the scroll
and found the place where it is written: 'The
Spirit of the Lord is upon me, because he has
anointed me to bring good news to the poor.
He has sent me to proclaim release to the captives and recovery of sight to the blind, to let
the oppressed go free, to proclaim the year of
the Lord's favour.' And he rolled up the scroll,
gave it back to the attendant, and sat down.
The eyes of all in the synagogue were fixed
upon him. Then he began to say to them, 'Today this scripture has been fulfilled in your
hearing.' All spoke well of him and were
amazed at the gracious words that came from
his mouth. They said, 'Is this not Joseph's
son?'

He said to them, 'Doubtless you will quote
to me this proverb, "Doctor, cure yourself!"
And you will say, "Do here also in your home

town the things that we have heard you did in Capernaum."' And he said, 'Truly I tell you, no prophet is accepted in the prophet's home town. But the truth is, there were many widows in Israel in the time of Elijah, when the heaven was shut up for three years and six months, and there was a severe famine over all the land; yet Elijah was sent to none of them except to a widow at Zarephath in Sidon. There were also many lepers in Israel in the time of the prophet Elisha, and none of them was cleansed except Naaman the Syrian.'

When they heard this, all in the synagogue were filled with rage. They got up, drove him out of town, and led him to the brow of the hill on which their town was built, so that they might hurl him off the cliff. But he passed through the midst of them and went on his way.

FILLED WITH RAGE
To proclaim release to captives

The Pilgrim

Black-eyed anger stalks through the house of my being. It strides about slamming doors and calling for blood. I tried to contain and control it, but it is too strong. I am afraid. I asked it who it was looking for.

My anger balled a fist and left one finger to accuse. It prodded my chest three times and said, 'You! I hate the way you are now. Your illness! I rage at the way it has stolen power and life. Your God! This God promised to release, heal and free! I shall throw this God off the nearest cliff.'

Hearing this I felt fear join us. Standing between anger and fear I asked, 'Am I fighting myself?' I already knew the answer. Fear moved closer and laid a hand on my shoulder. I felt its weight. My fear had grown bigger. My anger smiled sardonically and spoke loudly, 'Come forth my children.' I heard doors opening throughout my house and the sound of small feet. Small angers swarmed around our feet. 'I don't like the way people tell me it's all in the mind,' said one small voice. 'I don't like changing my plans all the time,' said another. Their voices grew with their number. Anger stood unmoving. Its children multiplied, their voices becoming more and more irrational. Behind me, fear's children began to appear and tug at my clothes—dozens of little anxieties I had forgotten. Who can save me? I am trapped in my own house.

Help me Lord. This struggle is an unequal contest. I am even becoming angry at my anger and afraid of my fear. Do not delay. The children are growing and soon it will not be anger and fear I stand between, it will be rage and panic.

Make haste and save me.

The Lord

Your anger is not your enemy: It points to the walls that imprison you. For so many years you have been your own architect. You sealed off this room, blocked those stairs and closed many windows. Your anger grows now because the interior you have built no longer serves you well.

Look behind your anger. You will see all the desires you have built into your home. You told yourself that each one was absolutely necessary for your well-being. So each room has only one way in and one way out. These walls seem unbreakable and the inner ways fixed. Reflect on it. Is perfect health absolutely essential for your well-being? Is perfect mobility? Is emotional control? Is freedom from all fear?

Consider my promises. What holds you captive the most? The reality of your illness or the desires you have walled around yourself? What blinds you the most? The realities of your limitations or the hatred you feel for a self that cannot measure up to unattainable expectations? What oppresses you the most? The light weight of the things you can do or the heavy weight of all the things you cannot do?

I am not your enemy. I will pass through the midst of your anger. With chronic illness it is enough to live with the natural anger that will come your way. Many of the irrational angers will pass away in time. As you begin to understand your desires the inner walls will fall.

Living room, play room, prayer room, resting room, treasure room and guest room will all be enlarged and open to each other. You will be released, free and able to see more clearly the things that really matter. There will be room enough for anger and laughter, for fear and hope. Who knows? In time there may be living spaces you have never dreamed of.

Prayer

Spirit of God anoint the house of my being. Help me to love my enemy, the fierce and powerful anger in me. Help me to accept all my feelings. Give me the courage to let them be.

Release me when I become captive to my own desires. Let me draw on the good energy that my desires bring and understand those that are not necessary for my well-being.

Restore my sight when I become blind to the walls I have built around myself. Help me to see there are many ways and possibilities in my life now. May the walls that imprison fall in their own time.

Free me when I become oppressed by the long lists of things I cannot do. Let me accept myself as I am now. Let me rejoice in what I can do.

When angers and fears multiply remind me that this is often so in times of illness. Even though they seem big now, let me remember that many will turn out to be false.

Above all, remind me to make no decisions during times like these.

May my own being become an open house full of light and good spirits. May it be a place big enough for all my feelings. May I feel at home in myself.

May you always feel welcome to come and stay.

Grief

Luke 7:11–15

Soon afterwards, Jesus went to a town called Nain, and his disciples and a large crowd went with him. As he approached the gate of the town, a man who had died was being carried out. He was his mother's only son, and she was a widow; and with her was a large crowd from the town.

When the Lord saw her, he had compassion for her and said to her, 'Do not weep.'

Then he came forward and touched the bier, and the bearers stood still. And he said, 'Young man, I say to you, rise!' The dead man sat up and began to speak, and Jesus gave him to his mother.

DO NOT WEEP

He touched the bier

The Pilgrim

Is it possible to grieve for yourself? My father
died many years ago and I know what grief is
like. Or rather, I knew then what and who I was
grieving for. Is it possible to grieve and not
know what it is that you have lost?

My grief is a changeling. It wears many faces.
It hides in heart spaces I thought were filled with
other feelings. Sometimes, when I am just resting
or feeling a bit sad, grief comes sounding up out
of my depths. Tears appear and catch me by surprise. I feel frightened. What have I lost that
makes me pine so deeply?

I make lists. My illness provides me with a
wealth of material. I have lost the ability to
work, lost my freedom to travel, lost energy to
socialise, lost health, lost concentration . . .
long lists, long enough for anyone to grieve.
But my lists do not help. I have begun to hear
a deep keening in my spirit. It is as if I have

lost myself. I feel appalled.

A friend said to me, 'Why are you so anxious? This disease is not life threatening.' But in another way it is life threatening. It threatens the way I live my life. It is killing the only way I know how to live life.

When I grieve it is as if I am attending my own funeral. As my illness gets worse I see my old self laid in a coffin. I grieve my own death. I carry my own coffin.

Like a widow who lost her only son, I have lost the one closest to me—my own self-image. I have lost myself. I have no other clothes to wear, no ready made image for myself who is chronically ill.

Tears come often now. A convalescent makes a poor spectacle in the procession of life. My face to the world has become my bier.

The Lord

Do not weep. I see your loss. The great glittering marvel of your self-image has not served you well over the years. And now, in your illness, it is like your worst fears have come true. You have neither the energy nor the luxury of maintaining such an image. I am not going to take you away to another place. You are grieving here, and here I grieve with you. Tears are in my eyes too.

See. I touch your bier. I recognise how much of you is in this. It is precious to me because you held it so close to yourself. Knowing you as I do, your self-image is a mix of many things. It is a mix of the beautiful and the gaudy, of the tender and the bravado, of generosity and greed, of the gift and the snare, of childhood trust and adulthood manipulation, of blessing and curse.

I touch this bier. Stand still now. You do not have to carry this coffin any further. I have come to give you life. You have lost a self image, but not yourself. The self at the heart of this bier is still alive. To this, to your true inner self, I say rise. Rise up! Go now to the nurturer of your heart.

Listen to your inner self speak. It will tell you how your old self image was crushing the life out of you. Look upon your inner self. It is always young and full of dreams. See the light on its face. Know now who was keening in the dark. You have not lost yourself—only some old clothes that no longer fit.

See how you stand now. Your inner self is tall and relaxed. Feel your whole body uncoil. Stretch your back muscles and breathe deeply, breathe right down into your inner self and it will breathe through you.

Prayer

Lord, a part of me has died. I grieve the loss. There is no greater attachment than the one to your own self-image. My loss is very real and no slight thing. The roots of my self-image reach deep into the sinew of my spirit. This illness has uncovered a keening that lacerates my heart. I wonder if I will ever be healed.

To be honest I was not ready for you to touch the bier. I thought that when you came to me you would take me away. I thought you would make everything better or at least make everything just the way it was before. How much would I have lost if I buried my heart's child with his clothes! I felt I was losing myself, and I was, but not to the grave. I have been mourning the loss of my self-image for so long that it seemed as if was losing myself.

Grieve with me, Lord. Let me see your tears. I have a lifetime of attachments and tears are still to come. Now I know why I grieve. How else to glean the precious in my self from the dross?

Later, I will thank you for freeing me. Later, I will rejoice in the new life you have nurtured. But for now I feel exposed. I feel both the soft light of your healing and the hard light of my illness. Send your Spirit to watch over me.

I am a chrysalis barely opened.

Illness

Luke 8:43–48

Now there was a woman who had been suffering from haemorrhages for twelve years; and though she had spent all she had on physicians, no one could cure her. She came up behind Jesus and touched the fringe of his clothes, and immediately her haemorrhages stopped.

Then Jesus asked, 'Who touched me?' When all denied it, Peter said, 'Master, it is the crowds that surround you and press in on you.' But Jesus said, 'Someone touched me for I noticed that power had gone out of me.'

When the woman saw that she could not remain hidden, she came trembling; and falling down before him, she declared in the presence of all the people why she had touched him, and how she had been immediately healed.

He said to her, 'Daughter, your faith has made you well; go in peace.'

WHO TOUCHED ME?

Your faith has made you well

The Pilgrim

Lord, you have become a stranger to me. I see you surrounded by others at church. I hear you spoken of by friends. I do not believe in a God of cheap healings. I am not sure I believe in healing at all. I should know, I have been sick for a very long time.

In the beginning I dragged out the prayers of my childhood. I pressed the saints for help. But as the months wore on and the years passed, I felt confirmed. If there is a God of healing, that God is no friend of mine. One has to face reality. I should know, I have been sick for a very long time.

Lord, you have never experienced chronic illness. Perhaps if you had, you would be no stranger to me. There is nothing like chronic illness. There is no plaster cast for friends to sign, no crystal ball for the doctors to tell me the course of my illness or the end of it. There are no infallible signs of recovery. Relapse is always waiting.

The only way to survive is acceptance. Long ago I locked my jaw and my heart. I have accepted the bleak reality of my body and yet still I bleed, still a wound weeps. I should know, I have been sick for a very long time.

In my mind's eye I see you surrounded by the crowds. They clamour and press around you. How sure their faith is! I wonder if they have bled for more than a day.

I see you, Lord, from the black rock pinnacle of my island. My reality comforts me. I have accepted it. Why do I still bleed? Why do I now feel uncertain?

I have no faith in healings, but perhaps if I can just touch the fringe of your clothes and leave, I will know if there is healing. I will know because I have been sick for a very long time.

The Lord

Who touched me? Please come forward. I have
been waiting for a long time to speak to you.
The bleeding has stopped. Your faith has made
you well. I see confusion in your eyes. Know
this: a faith that reaches out from a hard place is
greater than all the prayers that fill a church on
Sunday. It takes greater courage and risk. You
have to weigh the reality of your illness against
hope—and hope is real only in its absence. You
should know, you have been sick for a very long
time.

Do you know the source of your bleeding?
Perhaps it is the blood of a hundred small
wounds of disappointment. Perhaps it is a deep
wound—a past rejection, a betrayal of your love
or the loss of someone close. Perhaps it is the reality of your illness seeking a deeper acceptance.
You have been bleeding for a long time. I have
no cheap words. The bleeding has stopped. Let
go of the past. The wound itself will heal gently
in its own time—in your time.

Know this too: when you touched me, I was touched by you. You gave me the gift of your long suffering. You touched me in your weakness. When you touched me, I was aware of my own humanity—our shared need called down the healing love of our Creator. Thank you.

I have never experienced chronic illness, but you can tell me how it feels. You can whisper your fears and entrust your hopes to me. We could celebrate together the hard-won insights. We could give thanks for the help you have received from family, friends and doctors. How about it?

You have so much life in you, so much possibility. Let us set fires upon the beach of your island. Let us string up coloured lights and dig food pits. Light a beacon for passing ships. Your life could be a welcome port of call for other travellers. How about it, my friend?

Prayer

I never realised how close you were, my Lord. When I touched you I felt the healing begin. I never imagined you would want to share my weaknesses and my fears. I tried to put these things away.

I tried to 'accept' the frustration and alienation of my illness as a way of making them disappear. No matter how much I tried, I still felt a deeper bleeding, a wound that was never going to heal.

When I touched you, I discovered how much we share. I no longer feel alone. I can leave the black rock island I created for myself. The healing begins.

How freeing it is to know that I can share my suffering without embarrassment or guilt. I will light that beacon. I will try to welcome others into my life as you have welcomed me.

Best of all, my Lord, a small light with in me brightened when you told me that you are touched by me. It changes everything. I am impatient to see what will come of this.

Your love has begun to untie the bindings around my heart. Hope quickens in the very place where I was bleeding. I should know. I have been sick for a very long time.

Words

Luke 7:1–10

After Jesus had finished all his sayings in the hearing of the people, he entered Capernaum. A centurion there had a slave whom he valued highly, and who was ill and close to death. When he heard about Jesus, he sent some Jewish elders to him, asking him to come and heal his slave. When they came to Jesus, they appealed to him earnestly, saying, 'He is worthy of having you do this for him, for he loves our people, and it is he who built our synagogue for us.'

And Jesus went with them, but when he was not far from the house, the centurion sent friends to say to him, 'Lord do not trouble yourself, for I am not worthy to have you under my roof; therefore I did not presume to come to you. But only speak the word, and let my servant be healed. For I also am a man set under authority, with soldiers under me; and I say to one, "Go," and he goes, to another, "Come," and he comes, and to my slave, "Do this," and the slave does it.'

When Jesus heard this he was amazed at

him, and turning to the crowd that followed him, he said, 'I tell you, not even in Israel have I found such faith.'

When those who had been sent returned to the house, they found the slave in good health.

SPEAK THE WORD

Let my servant be healed

The Pilgrim

Only speak the word, Lord, and I shall be healed. Only speak the word. It is a little prayer. It fits on one breath. Yet, even as I say it now I wonder what I am asking for. The healing I desire has roots deeper than the physical reality of my illness. There is much within myself that is half-uncovered, half-sensed and half-lived. I see only dimly new beginnings, fresh shoots in the self, soil newly turned by my illness. I am driven to desire a deeper healing.

Once, in asking for your word, I sought the gentle word of presence in my suffering. I needed to feel you with me in the lonely hours, in the alienation that this illness seems to bring in its wake. At other times I sought a lover's word. I needed to feel that you loved me just as I was, fragile and vulnerable in my illness. I longed for a word of tenderness and compassion to fill the darkness within me.

I remember too, my Lord, the cries for help I made when I was sinking and helpless. Your word held my head above the waters. It was a near thing. I will never forget.

But now, in a quieter moment I sense my prayer is different. I wish I had the centurion's certainty. He was a leader and a soldier. I am neither. Yet I seek the same word he asked for—a word of power and authority. This is my prayer.

Only speak the word, Lord, the word that cracked light from the flint of darkness in the beginning of all creation. Speak the word that brooded over the waters and brought forth life in all its teeming variety. Speak the word that fell on your last breath as you died on the cross, the word that broke open tombs and quickened your Creator's hand to resurrect you. Only speak the word, the word of all power and authority, the word of life itself, and I shall be healed. Only speak the word!

The Lord

The centurion stands beside me now and smiles at your boldness. I too am gladdened beyond measure. Your long illness has brought you to deeper truths and to deeper longings. The whole court of heaven rejoices in your prayer. No longer do you seek healing for this ache or that pain. No longer do you curse the darkness with each relapse. Your half-sensed desire for deeper healing is a prayer for the word of life itself. Welcome to the mystery of your being.

'Only speak the word,' you pray. Know this: the healing you seek for your whole self has already begun. The word of power has already been spoken. The new creation that you half sense in yourself has started already. It began when you were only a small child held in your mother's and father's arms.

'When was this?' you wonder. I tell you that at your baptism the very waters of all creation were stirred and the Spirit of Life hovered above your head. When you were a child I made my home in you. Now I invite you to make your home in me. You are no longer a child. Only speak the word and I will heal you. Know this too: whenever I find such faith, my word leaps forth from the womb of the Creator's love.

When you seek this life, when you make your home in me, you will discover God. God's love is the life you seek. My life is God's word. I am the tenderness and compassion. I am God's word and you are my word. Do you understand?

You ask me to speak the word. When you live in me, your life is my word. When your life is broken and shared, my life is shared. When your life is celebrated, just as it is, my word becomes a light in the darkness. This is your healing. This is the way to find the life you seek.

You need not look for signs and wonders. Know this and write it in your heart: my word dances in your humanity!

Prayer

May the Lord's love blaze through me, catching up the small flame of my faith. May its light reach the darkest corners of my being. Warm me deep down, my Lord, deep down.

As a lover traces the vein on the back of a beloved's hand, so do you trace the lines of my life. I prayed for deep healing and you led me back to your first touch. Thank you for the grace of my baptism, for your Spirit's first breath on my forehead.

Help me now to grow in tenderness and compassion. May I become your word of healing to others. Where my life is broken, may it be shared so that the world may see the power of the Creator's love.

I blush that you would find a home in me. You have shown me how I may enjoy myself without miracle and marvel. Thank you.

May your word dance forever in mine.

Relapse

Luke 6:47-49

'Why do you call me "Lord, Lord" and do not do what I tell you? I will show you what someone is like who comes to me, hears my word, and acts on them.

That one is like a man building a house, who dug deeply and laid the foundation on rock; when a flood arose, the river burst against that house but could not shake it, because it had been well built.

But the one who hears and does not act is like a man who built a house on the ground without a foundation. When the river burst against it, immediately it fell, and great was the ruin of that house . . . '

NO FOUNDATIONS

Digging deep

The Pilgrim

I am completely washed out. I have hit rock bottom. The house of my hopes has been washed away. All my careful building has come to nothing. I have relapsed again.

I would rather be completely well or completely ill. At least then I would know where I stand. This constant building up and tearing down wears me out. Relapse follows relapse and here, amid the wreckage, I cannot even remember the good times.

I have tried to build myself up but the very earth shifts beneath me. When the waters flood I fall heavily and all my hopes fall with me. I am ruined. Is there any point in trying again?

I know sometimes I have done too much and brought on a relapse. I can accept this. Utterly devastating are the relapses I have no control over. These come just when I need the strength of a well-built house. These relapses leave me floundering in the ruins waiting for the waters to recede.

I have no control over life's seasons. I do not know when the waters will suddenly rise. I do not know if the ground under me will move or stay firm. I do not even know how long these relapses will last. All I do know is that with each relapse comes the deeper fear that I may never recover.

Lord, if you had an ounce of mercy you would not leave me to this fate. How many times have I recovered and built and prayed for healing? How many times have I cried in frustration and anger when everything is swept away?

I sit now in the ruins, mired in mud and black depression. Even the top soil has been carried away. Patches of bedrock show through the earth about me. They mock me at my worst saying, 'you have hit rock bottom again.'

The Lord

Why do you call me 'Lord' and not listen to my words? Why do you keep building on soil? You must know by now that the floods will always come. You will relapse.

I am glad that you have reached rock bottom. Now you have the chance to build your life on firm foundations. This is a grace of your illness—to have all the illusions swept away. You have been given new eyes to see that your old strengths, the timbers of your old life, were never truly strong. You have the chance to lay real foundations. But first you must dig deep.

It is painful to have illusions washed away. It is telling to discover the fragility of your own humanity. Yet it is the heart of your fragile, needy self that I love the most. It is where you are just yourself.

You may be surprised that your being like this is not as bad as you imagined. You no longer have to carry the weight of unattainable expectations. You are free from the fear of collapsing.

You no longer have to keep shoring up the timbers of your life. Let them go for now. Listen, act, dig deep and lay foundations.

If you dig deep you will find bare rock— you will find me. I do not care about performance or relapse. Build your foundations on me: one pillar of just action, one of tender love, one of humble trust and one of joyful thanks for the gift that you are. Bed these foundations on me and act upon them. Know that your dignity rests in you, just as you are, ill or well. Slowly your house will rise on firm foundations.

Few people ever have the chance that you have now. Be assured that at rock bottom I am bonded to you. As the masons of the past laid one stone, bridging the two below it, and called it a 'heart-bond', so my bond will be with you— a heart-bond of love. With this foundation you can quietly face every flood that life can bring against you.

Prayer

Lord be my rock and my foundation. When I relapse and all is swept away, let me feel the heart-bond of your love.

In my weakness and poverty let me build on your love and your strength. When I feel depressed and ruined by relapse, speak to me your words of life. Tell me again how precious I am before your eyes. When the river of life rises and bursts against me, hold me fast, deep down at my very foundations.

And if life is a river flooding through me, let your love too wash through me and flood my whole being.

Let your love bare the truth of my foundations—that, at rock bottom, I still have my dignity and the sure hope that you hold me close.

Through each relapse give me the courage and patience to dig deep.

Give me the faith to lay new foundations: to act justly, love tenderly and walk humbly with you, my God.

Chains
Luke 8:26–33, 38–39

Then they arrived at the country of the
Gerasenes, which is opposite Galilee. As Jesus
stepped out on land a man of the city who
had demons met him. For a long time he had
worn no clothes, and he did not live in a
house but in the tombs.

When he saw Jesus, he fell down before him
and shouted at the top of his voice, 'What
have you to do with me, Jesus, Son of the
Most High God? I beg you, do not torment
me.' For Jesus had commanded the unclean
spirit to come out of the man. (For many times
it had seized him; he was kept under guard
and bound with chains and shackles, but he
would break the bonds and be driven by the
demon into the wilds.) Jesus then asked 'What
is your name?' He said, 'Legion'; for many
demons had entered him. They begged him not
to order them to go back into the abyss.

Now there on the hillside a large herd of
swine was feeding; and the demons begged him
to let them enter these. So he gave them per-
mission. Then the demons came out of the man

and entered the swine, and the herd rushed down the steep bank into the lake and was drowned.

The man from whom the demons had gone begged that he might be with him; but Jesus sent him away, saying 'Return to your home, and declare how much God has done for you.'

LIFE IN THE TOMBS

I beg you, do not torment me

The Pilgrim

This disease has seized me and bound me up. I am prisoner, fettered in one place. So much freedom, energy and life has been taken from me. At least prisoners have a chance of parole, a shot at a reduced sentence. No such assurance for me. As my illness draws on, my life has become a life in the tombs. My friends draw away confused and embarrassed. I am alone. I feel lonely. I never expected to be in such a place.

What do you want of me, God? I prowl among the tombs of my past hopes and experiences. They are all dead, all gone. Now I have not even the energy to care. I read my own name on the tombstones that surround me. I hate this place, these fetters, this disease that has captured my body.

Nothing prepared me for this, the days stretch ahead and all I have is my anger. All I want to do is yell and tear at my body. I lift up my hands and stretch the chains taut. I feel the pull on my wrists, the weight of the reality of this disease. Each new little symptom adds another link.

I could cope if the 'demons' were outside me. I would gladly fight them with all my will, but they are inside me. I have lost heart. I fight myself. I exhaust myself. This disease feeds on the little energy I have. I am at an end. My friends tell me there is a look of half-hidden terror in my eyes. I feel so naked and vulnerable. Oh Lord, do not torment me!

The Lord

I hear your cry. I know this place. I have come. I too have been driven into the wilds and have been tested. I know what it is to feel helpless. I know what it is to have no power, no control at all. I have come to heal you. Be still. I give these demons leave to go.

Give me your hands. Show me the chains. Let me free you. Let me comfort you. I feel your anger. Good! You are alive! Give me your frustration and fear. Let it all pour out. These feelings will be with you in the future but they shall not chafe and bruise you. Let me heal the scars.

Come let us sit and chat. I see this is a place of many tombs. We need to stay here a while. Look around—some things are changed forever in your life. Some things are dead, gone forever. But you, my friend, you are free and alive.

You now know this wild dark place in your heart. Be assured of this; I will always be here to meet you. You need never be afraid of this place any more.

Let us walk together. This place is a part of you. In time you will accept this place without being seized with fear and anger, without hurting yourself.

Return to your home. Let the wounds of your heart heal in their own time. And remember, when you find another person afraid of this place, tell them what I have done for you.

Prayer

Lord, help me to accept the limitations of my life now. Help me to accept the reality of my illness. Give me the courage and faith to believe that I still have a life to live and enjoy.

When I feel angry and frustrated give me the grace to feel the strength of these feelings and then let them go. Help me to see that my feelings of anger and fear are signs of life. Do not let them chafe and bruise me. Help me to direct the energy to those things I can do.

Thank you for coming to me in the wilds. Thank you for sitting with me among the tombs. You have shown me that this place is a part of me. Knowing this and accepting this has made me whole.

You have loved me here among the tombs. Now I too can begin to love myself here. Thank you.

Help me to accept what is truly lost and to search out new opportunities for love and action. Let me love and savour the little I can do.

Heal the wounds of the past struggle. Break my chains. Draw the demons out into the light of day. Rest with me. Show me the way home.

Anxiety
Luke 12:22–31

Jesus said to his disciples, 'Therefore I tell you, do not worry about your life, what you will eat, or about your body, what you will wear. For life is more than food, and the body more than clothing.

'Consider the ravens: they neither sow nor reap, they have neither storehouse nor barn, and yet God feeds them. Of how much more value are you than the birds!

'And can any of you by worrying add a single hour to your span of life? If then you are not able to do so small a thing as that, why do you worry about the rest?

'Consider the lilies, how they grow: they neither toil nor spin; yet I tell you, even Solomon in all his glory was not clothed like one of these. But if God so clothes the grass of the field, which is alive today and tomorrow is thrown into the oven, how much more will he clothe you—you of little faith!

'And do not keep striving for what you are to eat and what you are to drink, and do not keep worrying. For it is the nations of the

*world that strive after all these things, and
your Father knows that you need them.*

*'Instead, strive for his kingdom, and these
things will be given to you as well . . . '*

DO NOT WORRY
Your Father knows your needs

The Pilgrim

It is time, my Lord, to stop. I cannot take another step. I have had it. The burdens I carry are too much. I am yoked to my life's worries. Each day anxiety adds another load.

I feel like a beast of burden under a harsh caravan master. I worry about health and he adds the burden of performance. I worry about performance and he adds the burden of the future. I worry about the future and he adds the burden of the past. I worry about the past and he adds the burden of the present. I worry about the present and he adds the burden of change. I worry about change and he adds the burden of keeping control. Anxiety is crushing me. It is the never-ending weight upon weight, worry upon care, load upon burden and stress upon stress.

My task master has hard eyes. The whip never leaves his hand. His true face is always hidden. The mask of my anxiety is a face frozen into the look of supreme control. Its lips carve in an apologetic smile. Every line seems to say, 'I am sorry, but you must understand that I have a job to do. You will forgive me if I have to use the whip.'

In desperation, Lord, I clawed the mask of anxiety and found a more terrible face—the teeth-bared face of anger. But it too was a mask. Under it I found the wide-eyed mask of fear. And under fear lay the scarred face of memory. Under memory I caught a glimpse of the tear-lined mask of grief. Perhaps under grief lies my true face, but I will never know.

For the defeating truth of anxiety is that one of the loads I carry is a bag of masks. Whenever my left hand unmasks, my right hand reaches for another mask. I am powerless. Do you know now, Lord, why I worry about my life?

The Lord

Come to me. My yoke is easy and my burden is light. I love you—masks, anxieties and all. Do not be troubled or afraid. I can see your true face. And I love what I see.

Your true face is not terrible. It is not worse than being a beast of burden. Do you want to be driven by anxiety forever? For five more years? One year? A month? Another day? How long before one more load will break your back?

I can see your true face. How it longs to be free! How it yearns to embrace the dumb beast!

Between your true face and the weary life you have chosen lie the masks. And in each mask, in each carved detail, lies the power of your own feelings. Each mask is the work of a lifetime. Anger, fear and grief are not illusions. There is nothing false in these masks. You cannot hope to rip them off with quick courage and be set free. Your right hand will defeat the left until the day anxiety itself lays down the masks.

Rest both your hands. Put them in mine. Let

us sit together with anxiety until the first mask is revealed. It matters not what it shows. Let us sit with each mask in turn. Let us contemplate each feature and trace the lines of your feelings. And when healing is found, we will rejoice to see anxiety drop the masks it no longer needs.

I will heal you. My kingdom can be found now. It is not in the past or the future, not in performance or control, not in good health or clothes or any of the things you worry about.

My kingdom is found in every person who wears their true face. My kingdom grows in the world when the masks of exploitation, greed and oppression are laid aside. My kingdom is the slow dawning of every person's full worth and dignity.

Strive for the kingdom and the rest will be given to you.

Prayer

Lord I am full of anxiety. I cannot see the end of it. My worries overburden me. I am driven before the whip of my anxiety. Free me from this merciless task master.

I know that worry does not change anything, yet I worry. I need you to remind me of the love of my family and friends. I need the assurance of love without conditions or judgement. I need their love and your love. I need to be sure that you already love my true face before the unmasking.

If you would sit with me, if you would shoulder my burdens for a while, I could hope to be free. I would be willing to seek my true face. I could begin to seek your kingdom.

Lord, in you I am God-found. You know my needs. Hold me safe as I discover them. Hold me gently as I come to know each mask. Hold me in the dance when each mask falls away. Hold me close when I come to see the true face of my inner being.

And when I am Self-found, let me join you in knowing the needs of others.

Despair

Luke 5:1–11

Once while Jesus was standing beside the lake of Gennesaret, and the crowd was pressing in on him to hear the word of God, he saw two boats there at the shore of the lake; and the fishermen had gone out of them and were washing their nets. He got into one of the boats, the one belonging to Simon, and asked him to put a little way out from the shore. Then he sat down and taught the crowds from the boat.

When he had finished speaking, he said to Simon, 'Put out into the deep water and let down your nets for a catch.' Simon answered, 'Master, we have worked all night long but have caught nothing. Yet if you say so, I will let down the nets.'

When they had done this, they caught so many fish that their nets were beginning to break. So they signalled their partners in the other boat to come and help them. And they came and filled both boats, so that they began to sink.

But when Simon Peter saw it, he fell down

at Jesus' knees, saying, 'Go away from me, Lord, for I am a sinful man!' For he and all who were with him were amazed at the catch of fish that they had taken; and so were James and John, sons of Zebedee, who were partners with Simon.

Then Jesus said to Simon, 'Do not be afraid; from now on you will be catching people.' When they had brought their boats to shore, they left everything and followed him.

INTO DEEP WATER
We have caught nothing

The Pilgrim

To throw out your nets and to come up empty is a disappointment. To come up empty when you make your living as a fisherman is a disappointment and a worry. To use every skill you have learnt in your life and still to come up empty is to know disappointment and self-doubt. To return to shore empty is to know a small despair.

In this, Lord, I feel close to Simon Peter the fisherman. Many times during this illness I have tried to find life and have come up empty-handed. I have tasted the edge of despair's shadow. I have known emptiness where there used to be life. In long nights I have spent my strength fishing for meaning, for some small understanding of my life. Slumped down in my body, my spirit finds only despair.

In the days following these times I walk a little way down despair's road and see the edge of the pit. It is not a pleasant place to be. It is not a place for tarrying too long. In the pit lies a great despair. I have not been taken that far but I have discovered that even a small despair is a jealous master. It will not abide distractions. It wants all of me.

I know why Simon Peter made no objection to your use of his boat. He would hardly have been aware of your presence as he brooded over his night's empty work. He would not have heard a word of what you were saying to those gathered on shore. Despair, even a small despair, is not interested in speeches. And when you sent Simon out into the deeps again, the act of throwing out the nets could only have been an act of futility.

So it seems to me every time I bring before you the empty deeps of my life. Only the fear of a great despair moves me. Still I will lower the nets once more.

The Lord

Have you ever wondered why I choose to stand in your boat to speak about life? Have you grasped the irony of my choice? Yours is an empty boat and you are a fisherman who cannot catch fish! Did you notice that I found my footing in your empty nets? Why do you think I insist that you return to the deeps—to the very place where all your skills and hard work came to nothing? Why am I asking you to risk empty nets again?

I am the author of extravagant life! I break empty nets with abundance beyond all expectation. You need hope and I cannot give you that on the shore. We have to return to the deeps. I can make no promises—that would defeat hope. I can only ask you to throw out the nets again. I can only trust my presence will encourage you to act.

I will not help. I cannot lay a hand on those nets. Do you understand that you have to do this yourself? Do you understand that Peter's action was not an act of futility? You are wrong about that. The very moment you act in the face of no hope, you act in hope!

So many people speak about hope. What they really mean is expectation or desire or want or need. None of these is hope. Hope is the only gift that must necessarily be found in the experience of its absence. Otherwise it is not true hope. And very often it is not a feeling but an action in the face of a feeling. That feeling is not disappointment or anxiety. It is the full weight of despair. To act in the face of this feeling is to hope.

Hope only appears in its absence. Hope is not lost with the feeling of despair. It is lost when you can no longer act—when you physically become lifeless.

So come, return to the deeps. Invite me into your empty boat. Lower your nets. Hope!

Prayer

Lord, break open the nets of my despair. Draw up from the depths of my being the abundance of life that is within me. Come to me in my bone-tired weariness and despair. Take me back over the deeps where I have found no life and bid me act again. Show me how to hope.

When I find myself despairing, let me know your presence. When I feel that I am at the end of my strength, when there is no point in trying any longer, let me hear your voice. When life seems empty and I begin to doubt myself, give me the gift of hope. Let me act for life and for living in the face of its absence.

Remind me that even one small action for life is an act of hope. Each of these small acts gathers vitality in those places where I have found only emptiness.

When you call me let me answer, sure in the knowledge that you wish to draw a catch in the deeps of my life. You wish to feed the hungry and hope is a catch to be shared. Give me the courage to share my hope with others.

Lord, stand in the empty nets of my life. You are my hope. When we are done I know you will leave me standing waist-deep in glistening, silver-flashing, teeming life.

Panic

Luke 23:33–46

When they came to the place that is called The Skull, they crucified Jesus there with the criminals, one on his right and one on his left. Then Jesus said, 'Father, forgive them; for they do not know what they are doing.' And they cast lots to divide his clothing.

And the people stood by, watching; but the leaders scoffed at him, saying, 'He saved others; let him save himself if he is the Messiah of God, his chosen one!' The soldiers also mocked him, coming up and offering him sour wine, and saying, 'If you are the King of the Jews, save yourself!' There was also an inscription over him, 'This is the King of the Jews.'

One of the criminals who were hanged there kept deriding him and saying, 'Are you not the Messiah? Save yourself and us!' But the other rebuked him, saying, 'Do you not fear God, since you are under the same sentence of condemnation? And we indeed have been condemned justly, for we are getting what we deserve for our deeds, but this man has done nothing wrong.' Then he said, 'Jesus, remem-

ber me when you come into your kingdom.' He replied, 'Truly I tell you, today you will be with me in Paradise.'

It was now about noon, and darkness came over the whole land until three in the afternoon, while the sun's light failed; and the curtain of the temple was torn in two.

Then Jesus, crying with a loud voice, said, 'Father, into your hands I commend my spirit.' Having said this, he breathed his last.

THE SUN'S LIGHT FAILED

Save us and save yourself

The Pilgrim

Blood rushes to my face. I catch my breath. I know what is coming. My muscles spasm. Panic spills over my head and it feels like boiling water. Wave after wave scalds down my face. It runs into my eyes and down my throat. It breaks across my chest and arms. Every pore in my skin is alive with pain. Then suddenly it is gone. I breathe again. Until next time.

Panic holds my body captive. With each attack the pain of a thousand tiny needles breaks across the crown of my head. I do not know why I am afflicted with this pain. I do not know what sets it off. Even when I am suffering panic I look in the mirror and there is nothing to see: no rash, no torn skin, no blood, no scar. So much pain and nothing to see for it.

I am not a person who panics in a crisis. I panic now but I am not panicky. What is going on inside me? It comes even when I am quietly talking to a friend. I have no power to stop it. Panic holds me hostage. I do not know the ransom.

All of this is on top of my illness. Already I am utterly fatigued. Already I have all the other symptoms of my disease. I cannot walk a dozen metres. I cannot burn the adrenalin out of my body. I do not have the energy.

It is all I can do to hold on to the support of my friends. They are wordless like me. I have interrogated my thoughts, my mind and my heart. The strong one within mocks me. Another part of me is enraged with the sick one. Neither of them has any answers and they are starting to turn on each other.

I am close to despair. My God, why do you not save me? The sun's light has failed. Darkness has covered my life. The curtain of my faith has been torn in two.

There is only one thing left for me. I will throw myself on your mercy.

The Lord

Look at me. Blood has congealed in my face. I catch my breath. I know what is coming. My arms cannot take the weight of my body for long. My muscles spasm. Wave after wave of pain runs down my arms and ribs. Every pore in my skin is alive with pain. Then the spasms stop. I breathe again. Until next time.

Look at me. My body is racked on a cross. My head too is crowned with thorns. I need no mirror. Torn skin and blood disfigure my whole body. Yet none of my disciples or friends know why this has come to pass. Most have fled in terror. So much pain and nothing to see for it.

Look at me. I am crucified. My pain comes while I try to talk quietly to my own mother. I am held hostage to the fear and panic of the authorities. I could have been ransomed, but my own people choose Barabbas. Who will ransom me now?

Look at me. My hands and feet are nailed to wood. My shoulders and back were already torn by the whip. My body is utterly fatigued. I cannot even walk one step. I do not have the energy. I do not have the choice.

Look at me. Listen. The soldiers and the people interrogate me. They mock my past strengths. They all want answers. If I am God's son why do I not save myself? The two crucified on either side of me have turned on each other. One is angry and one sees my innocence.

Look at me. I am close to despair. My God, why have you forsaken me? The sun's light has failed. Darkness has covered the whole land. The curtain of the temple is torn in two.

There is only one thing left for me. Father, into your hands I commend my spirit.

Prayer

Face to face, my Lord. Mine to yours. Hands to hands. Muscles to muscles. Blood to blood. Arms to arms. Skin to skin. Feet to feet. Body to body. Heart to heart.

Cross to cross, my Lord. Mine in yours. Nail to nail. Suffering to suffering. Thorns to thorns. Pain to pain.

Ransom to ransom, my Lord. Mine through yours. Mocking to mocking. Anger to anger. Innocence to innocence. Despair to despair.

Darkness to darkness, my Lord. Mine and yours. Powerlessness to powerlessness. Waiting to waiting. Unknowing to unknowing. Mystery to mystery.

Prayer to prayer, my Lord. Mine with yours. Cry to cry. Spirit to spirit. Son to Father. Me to you.

Death to death, my Lord. Yours in mine.

Death to life, my Lord. Yours for mine.

Life to life, my Lord. Mine in yours.

Death

Luke 8:40–42, 49–55

Now when Jesus returned, the crowd welcomed him, for they were all waiting for him. Just then there came a man named Jairus, a leader of the synagogue. He fell at Jesus' feet and begged him to come to his house, for he had an only daughter, about twelve years old, who was dying. While Jesus was still speaking, someone arrived from the leader's house to say, 'Your daughter is dead; do not trouble the teacher any longer.' When Jesus heard this, he replied, 'Do not fear. Only believe, and she will be saved.'

When he came to the house, he did not allow anyone to enter with him, except Peter, John, and James, and the child's father and mother. They were all weeping and wailing for her; but he said, 'Do not weep; for she is not dead but sleeping.' And they laughed at him, knowing she was dead. But he took her by the hand and called out, 'Child, get up!' Her spirit returned, and she got up at once. Then he directed them to give her something to eat.

SHE IS NOT DEAD

Her spirit returned and she got up

The Pilgrim

I dreamed, my Lord, that a child had died. When I awoke I felt a great loss. This long illness has taken so much from me. I've lost my freedom, my energy, my old life and my good spirits. I have lost the desire to make the best of it and the hope of a quick recovery. I am afraid there is worse to come.

Last night I dreamed about the child within me. I was surprised. I had long outgrown and forgotten her. She cried out to me. She told me she was dying. I looked upon her and I saw she was dead. In the morning I grieved. My dream was a messenger come to tell me my child was dead.

Lord, the heart has gone out of my life. A light somewhere deep inside has blown out. I feel a hollow place, a scary place. A darkness is growing in me. As my illness takes my body, piece by piece, my spirit dies inside. It is all too much.

Oh, I can keep a brave face. I can scatter brittle-bright words for those around me. But inside it is as though a child has died. This more than anything else defeats me.

I have no more words, no more prayers. You have come too late, my Lord. I will no longer trouble you.

The Lord

Do not be afraid. She will be safe. I have come.
Would I be absent when you rediscover one of
the great gifts of your life?

How long is it since you felt the lightness of
your being? How long is it since laughter burst
from your belly? When did you lose your sense
of the ridiculous? Have you noticed how hard
your sense of play has to work? Your grand
plans, your life's worries, your headlong chase
for security and power have cost you too much.
How long since you felt like doing nothing or
enjoying the present moment like a child? How
long is it since you felt the child within? How
long is it since you cared for her, complemented
her, gave her the lead in your life—or at least
equal time? You have lost something very precious. You do well to grieve.

Your illness has torn away all the masks. This
is a gift. You begin to see again—to see all that I
created in you. Without this suffering, this sudden
change in your life, you would never have heard

the faint cries of your child. She has been struggling. She is only a child, but she owes her well-being, her life to you.

Come. Let us enter the house of your being. Look upon the child within. Feel your grief. Feel your loss. She looks dead, but she is asleep. She is alive.

Go to your child now. Hug her, hold her close. Take your time to get to know her again. Take time to listen to her. Indulge her, pamper her—feel the light inside being rekindled. Let the delight of her presence shine through your body. Let it animate you and heal you. She will walk with you through the dark hollow places and run with you in the single joys of your life now. Watch over her as you get better—do not leave her behind. Do not forget her. Lift her high on your shoulders—she is a light and easy burden. Stop crying. She is alive.

Now, give her something to eat. Nourish her.

Prayer

Lord, I rejoice that the child within me is alive. I was so afraid. I know what I nearly lost. Let me never forget her or leave her behind again.

Her healing is my healing. The light in her eyes shines in my eyes. She is full of dance and rhyme. My heart is greened and my spirit runs like wild flowers across the high plains.

The spirit of play returns, the spirit of wonder has come back to me. The spirit of laughter bubbles through the house of my being. In my illness I had shut them out. Now they gather around me. The child within has brought many playmates.

The spirit of trust stands behind me and the spirit of creativity is at my side. The spirit of the absurd awaits my pleasure. The spirit of the imaginable has just thrown me a kiss and the spirit of young dreams offers me her arms.

The spirit of doing nothing is at my feet. The spirit of wasting time is tugging at my clothes. Like young children they want my attention. I see too that the spirit of follies and crazy projects is impatient to get going again. The child within has returned.

She is alive and sits on my shoulders. Thank you Lord for bringing us together again.

Time

Luke 5:12–13

Once, when Jesus was in one of the cities, there was a man covered with leprosy. When he saw Jesus he bowed with his face to the ground and begged him, 'Lord, if you choose, you can make me clean.' Then Jesus stretched out his hand, touched him, and said, 'I do choose. Be made clean.' Immediately the leprosy left him.

LORD, IF YOU CHOOSE
I do choose

The Pilgrim

Lord, if you really want to, you can heal me.
Why do you delay? I know you are with me in
my illness. I have felt a gentle ease during difficult times. I believe you care. So why do you
take so long to heal me? It is as if you are just
standing there doing nothing. I am left waiting.
Do you know what waiting means for one who
has a chronic illness?

In the early days of my illness I believed I
would get better in a couple of months. I believed you would heal me. Later I measured my
illness by the year. But I discovered there is
nothing magic about one year or two or three.

I found there was nothing magic about any
measure of time I cared to make, and I did mark
off time: I would improve by my birthday, by
Christmas, by the weekend, after a good night's
sleep, after a big relapse, when I could exercise
a little, when a friend with the same illness re-

covered, after a visit to the specialist, after three good days, after winter, after peaceful prayer.

Of course the reality of chronic illness is that one might get better, one might get worse or one might be the same. It is difficult to count on any thing or any time. I have found I cannot even say this time will be like the last time. This time with friends or this time of relapse or recovery may be very different from the last time. Sometimes a sleepless night can feel like a week. At other times months can disappear like a fine summer's day. In illness time wields a heavier and sharper blade.

I used to tell others to take each day as it comes. Good advice, but have you ever tried? Have you ever been forced to live one day at a time, without carrying anything from the past or counting on anything for the morrow? I find this enormously difficult. Time itself has begun to pester me. It asks if perhaps you do not choose to heal me.

The Lord

My friend, I am not a carnival spruiker offering side-show marvels on the half-hour. I am not a children's lucky dip where you pay your money and every draw is a winner. I am not a course of medication or part of a recipe for a six-minute meal. I am a person just like you.

When you speak to me I listen. I know your name and I know you. I have always desired to know you better. Before I do anything else I want to touch you. I want to give you time to touch me. Relationships of any worth take time.

I hear your prayer. Before I act I want you to hear my answer. I want you to hear my affirmation: 'I want to heal you. I do choose to heal you.' Let these words sit in your belly. Relish them, taste them, breathe them deep into your lungs and enjoy them.

In healing, time is not your enemy. It is your friend. In healing, your whole life can be a prayer. In healing our relationship will change. It takes time to heal life's hurts, to discover the idols in your life and to let go of the false images you have of me. Time is your friend and, in your illness, it can be a special grace.

While you wait for healing, see the hand I hold over you. In the long hours, when time stretches out, feel my touch. I too am uncertain of our relationship in these times. My touch will be tentative and gentle. We both face an unknown future. In time we may begin to trust each other. Then you will find it easier to live each day as it comes.

Love and trust and hope all take time. Why should you think healing is any different? I do not accuse or blame or torture my friends. You need not be so violent with yourself. I do choose to heal you.

Please give us the time for exploring each other. Give us time together without agendas and expectations. Give us time for words of love. In this time comes healing.

Prayer

I thank you Lord that you have chosen to care for me. From my mother's womb you have known me, but I have been slow to know you. Help me to understand the false idols in my life. Help me to see the false images I have of you. Let us meet one another as we really are right now.

I want you to heal me. Even more, I desire to feel your hand over me. I want to feel your touch in the difficult times and the blessed times, in health and in sickness. Give me the patience and courage to let our relationship grow and deepen. Free me from the expectations that blind or twist or destroy. Let us learn to sit gently with each other. I know you want only the very best for me.

Let me hear over and over again your words of affirmation and love. Help me to live fully each day as it comes. Help me to discover what may be for me this day.

And when your healing is done may I give

thanks not only for the healing, but also for the healer. You, my Lord and my God, have healed me. You have come into my life. I am happy.

You are a friend and a companion for all times.

Prayer
Luke 11:5–13

Jesus said to them, 'Suppose one of you has a
friend, and you go to him at midnight and say
to him, "Friend, lend me three loaves of
bread; for a friend of mine has arrived and I
have nothing to set before him." And he answers from within, "Do not bother me; the
door has already been locked, and my children
are with me in bed; I cannot get up and give
you anything."

'I tell you, even though he will not get up
and give him anything because he is his friend,
at least because of his persistence he will get
up and give him whatever he needs.

'So I say to you: Ask, and it will be given
you; search, and you will find; knock, and the
door will be opened for you. For everyone who
asks receives, and everyone who searches finds,
and for everyone who knocks, the door will be
opened.

'Is there anyone among you who, if your
child asks for a fish, will give a snake instead
of a fish? Or if the child asks for an egg, will
give a scorpion?

'If you then, who are evil, know how to give good gifts to your children, how much more will the heavenly Father give the Holy Spirit to those who ask him!'

ASK, SEARCH, KNOCK
The door will be opened

The Pilgrim

I woke in the middle of the night. Wrestling with demons, running with legs that would not carry me. My dreams exhaust me, Lord. Again I prayed to you. Again you did not answer.

My life is a landscape of endless mountains. I climb. I fall. I regather energy. I climb again. I fall again. I cry to you for healing. You do not answer. I persist and climb again. I fall again. Why do you not answer? I have knocked on the door of your heart till my hands are bloody. That door has not opened. Will you make a mockery of your promises? Am I so worthless? Am I to be thrown aside from your sight?

In the early days of my illness I trusted you. In time, I told my heart, in God's own time I will find healing. I prayed each day and told myself tomorrow would be better. But it was not better. I swallowed frustration, thanked you for my faith and hid my desperation. Next month would see me right. Not so. Then it came to me. Perhaps if I stopped climbing mountains you would rescue me. Yes. I was at peace. I waited. I trusted for another month. No word from you, Lord, no healing. Each day my teeth clench a little tighter and each day my anger grows.

When I seek to reassure my heart in the early hours of the morning, my anger strides about my room wanting to break and smash. It grows and feeds on your silence. Are you listening? Ask, you say, and I will receive! I have asked, damn you, till my voice grows dry. I have pleaded, begged, cried, shouted and banged on your door. Are you a liar as well as deaf? I have been faithful for months. What more do you want! There has been not a crumb of bread from your almighty hands. Your words are ashes in my mouth. If you stood before me now I would smash your face open. You are nothing but a dealer in scorpions and snakes. Come. Answer me.

The Lord

Be still, and know that I am God.

Prayer

'Be still and know that I am your God.' I am speechless. I am undone. I can still feel my anger. I still want to fight, but your words disarm me.

I was ready to demand account for each and every prayer unanswered. You call me to stillness and faith. I was going to point out how I was a good person and deserved better. You ask for stillness and trust. I had held your words in the bible ready to accuse you in the stand. You guide me to stillness and the certainty that you are my God.

In the time I have been sick I have begged for healing to a thousand hurts. My desires and needs were honed sharp. I placed each before you. You gave me silence and you ask for silence. Now I see.

I mistook silence and stillness for emptiness. In that silence, a little way apart from my anger and suffering, I found you waiting. You have not asked me to feel any different. You only ask me to join you in the stillness. I am speechless. It is well. There are no words, just you and me, as I am and as you are.

Strangely, peace is here. In the mess of my life all is well. My prayer is this Lord: you are my God. Hold me in the stillness of your being.

Compassion
Luke 15:11–24

Then Jesus said, 'There was a man who had two sons. The younger of them said to his father, "Father, give me the share of the property that will belong to me." So he divided his property between them. A few days later the younger son gathered all he had and travelled to a distant country, and there he squandered his property in dissolute living.

When he had spent everything, a severe famine took place throughout that country, and he began to be in need. So he went and hired himself out to one of the citizens of that country, who sent him to his fields to feed the pigs. He would gladly have filled himself with the pods that the pigs were eating; and no one gave him anything.

But when he came to himself he said, "How many of my father's hired hands have bread enough and to spare, but here I am dying of hunger! I will get up and go to my father, and I will say to him, 'Father, I have sinned against heaven and before you; I am no longer worthy to be called your son; treat me like one of your hired hands.'"

So he set off and went to his father. But while he was still far off, his father saw him and was filled with compassion; he ran and put his arms around him and kissed him. Then the son said to him, "Father, I have sinned against heaven and before you; I am no longer worthy to be called your son."

But the father said to his slaves, "Quickly, bring out a robe—the best one—and put it on him; put a ring on his finger and sandals on his feet. And get the fatted calf and kill it, and let us eat and celebrate; for this son of mine was dead and is alive again; he was lost and is found!"

And they began to celebrate . . . '

TO BE IN NEED

He came to himself

The Pilgrim

When I came to myself, Lord, I was perishing with hunger. I was starving for a sense of meaning, for a deep assurance that you loved me. The ribs of my faith showed stark in the skin of my self-understanding.

The journey of my life has taken me to faraway lands. I kept my faith but the riches you gave me, all my personal gifts, I have squandered on useless things. I used them to impress myself, to fulfil my own agenda, to earn admiration and to meet the expectations of others. When I became ill I lost the use of most of my gifts. So when the great famine arose in my life I was famished. The distance between us was great. I was shocked by the gauntness of my spirit.

In the rich years my life was filled with much activity. With my strengths I centred my living in work, in short-term goals, in whims and worries.

I had a hundred distractions. In the lean years, my spirit began to hunger; I came to be in need. I came to hunger for my humanity.

Now I find myself on the road back to you, Lord. I see you from afar and I feel the poverty of my heart. I have wasted my energy and gifts in faraway places. I want to come home. I want to come home to myself and to you, to the original embrace of your love and your will.

As I feel the end of a long road in the soles of my bare feet, I wonder if you will be angry. I wonder if you will demand penance. I wonder if my illness was some kind of natural justice.

In the rhythm of my feet, I pound out my prayer, 'I am unworthy to be called your son, I am lost. I am hungry, I am sorry, I am unworthy.'

In the rhythm of my heart, I beat out my need—a sense of a place before you, a sense of harmony, a sense of wholeness, a sense of mission, a sense of thanksgiving, a sense of being open to love.

In the rhythm of my hope and need, I can hardly believe my eyes. Is that really you running towards me?

The Lord

When you came to yourself I felt you come to
me. I saw you from afar. I felt your loss and confusion. I saw you squander some of your riches,
and I rejoiced when you set your feet towards
me. My heart goes out before me. As you draw
closer I feel the passion of your suffering.

I am full of passion with you. My compassion
reaches for you. I longed to speak to you before
this, but you could not hear me. I saw you
spend the riches of your humanity on many
things that did not make you happy. I saw you
use your gifts for power and control. I felt some
of your most precious dreams die. I saw opportunities lost because you were unable to see past
your own plans. I saw wilfulness and selfish-
ness. I saw anxiety and blindness as you sought
to shape a place in the world where you felt
secure. All the while you were becoming poor.

Even so, I never stopped loving you. I loved
you when you were born. I loved you when you
went on your own way. I loved you when you

felt the pinch, and I grieved when the famine struck. I waited as the gaunt face of your spirit began to speak to your heart. I never stopped loving you.

Now I see you clearly. Do not walk any faster. I will come to you. I have already forgotten the past. Let me hug and kiss you.

Here. Take this cloak. Put on these shoes. I know you are uncomfortable with these clothes. You do not realise it now, but the brother of your heart is resentment. A part of you is angry with my easy forgiveness. It wants punishment. But I am full of compassion. I want to drink and feast and tell everyone you are back home. I want to celebrate.

Come. We will make merry today because you were lost and now you are found. You were dead and now you are alive.

Prayer

Lord, I did not deserve it, yet I was truly glad to feel your arms around me. At last my spirit rests because knowing my want, I now know what to ask for. Knowing your welcome, I now know you will spare me nothing.

You clothe me in love and forgiveness. You wrap me in a cloak of compassion. A ring of fidelity you place on my finger. You will never desert me. Your shoes set my feet on the right road. You clear away all obstacles before me.

You call for the fatted calf. You spend all to celebrate my return. None of this have I earned. None of this do I deserve. All of this I have longed for in my need. Thank you.

I feel guilty. A part of me wants justice and payment for folly. But your justice is not mine. You are impatient to restore all that I thought was lost. You return to me all that I have squandered.

When you embraced me I felt all the riches of my humanity. When you kissed me I felt all the special gifts you have given me awaken.

I pray now that, in the healing, I may begin to live in love and truth.

I pray that, ill or well, my life will be fully directed towards your will for me. I look forward to my part in your kingdom of mercy and justice.

I pray that I will always find you in the fatted calf, the merry-making of my God with me, in all the circumstances of my life.

In your compassionate welcome, Lord, I am found.

Surprise

Luke 24:1–12

But on the first day of the week, at early dawn, the women came to the tomb, taking the spices that they had prepared. They found the stone rolled away from the tomb, but when they went in, they did not find the body.

While they were perplexed about this, suddenly two men in dazzling clothes stood beside them. The women were terrified and bowed their faces to the ground, but the men said to them, 'Why do you look for the living among the dead? He is not here, but has risen. Remember how he told you, while he was still in Galilee, that the Son of Man must be handed over to sinners, and be crucified, and on the third day rise again.' Then they remembered his words, and returning from the tomb, they told all this to the eleven and to all the rest.

Now it was Mary Magdalene, Joanna, Mary the mother of James, and the other women with them who told this to the apostles. But these words seemed to them an idle tale, and they did not believe them.

But Peter got up and ran to the tomb; stooping and looking in, he saw the linen cloths by themselves; then he went home, amazed at what had happened.

AMAZEMENT
He saw the linen cloths

The Pilgrim

It pays to check the tomb, my Lord. With chronic
illness healing comes so slowly that you tend to
consign certain freedoms and energies to the
grave forever. After nearly two years I found myself reliving some of the worst times. Gut-
clenched, I expected to feel the same hopeless-
ness and pain. But, to my surprise, it was not so.

The memories were still clear, but the corpse
of lost hopes had vanished. The sense of death
and grief had left. Some of the weight of this illness had lifted and I felt like running home to
tell all of my friends.

It pays to check the tomb. So many experiences, so many loves and enjoyment I had left
there, each one spice-wrapped and bound to
trap the smell of failure and loss.

So imagine my surprise when I found the
tomb was empty! All that remained were the
binding cloths, neatly folded and left to one side.

It makes me wonder, Lord, what other surprises you have for me. In what other places have you quietly healed while I have been caught up in my illness? It makes me wonder if the healing began long ago. How long have I been grieving over an empty tomb?

Surprise not only catches the breath, it widens the eyes. I begin to see better now. I begin to see the times when I did not relapse. I see the times when I was able to listen to another who suffered. I see the time when I could rest happily through a bad patch. Lord, I could go on—and that itself is a surprise!

What life have you won for me? Dare I return to the tomb again? What else have I consigned to the grave? What else might be given new life?

It is not just finding an empty tomb, but the feeling that, newly risen, you wait just out of sight ready to surprise me yet again.

And that, Lord, feels just great!

The Lord

Why do you look for the living among the dead?

I am alive . . . and so are you. I am the same but different . . . so are you. After my resurrection it took time for my friends to recognise me. So it will be for you. It will even take time for you to recognise yourself.

Everyone loves a surprise. You were made in my image. You only have the capacity for surprise because your God has it in greater measure. Surprise me! Surprise yourself! As Peter bent down breathless to look into the tomb, stoop and look into your own heart. You will be surprised. Let your life surprise others. Let my word in you surprise the world.

Empty tombs will always surprise. Yours is no different from mine. People will wonder if your illness was such a bad thing, or even if you were really ill at all. Others will wonder if they too can hope for life in their dying. Such is your faith.

We will both carry the scars—healed scars. Such is the pattern of our humanity when gathered by our God's love. Such is our faith.

Know this: the surprise of healing turns accountants into clowns. The surprise of life in death turns mausoleums into maternity wards. The surprise of my presence turns on my love . . . and my love will never end. Such is my faith.

Do not forget this moment. Remember your surprise. Remember the sudden dance of grace in your being. Remember how your eyes were opened. Remember where it happened. Then you will not be so quick to bury the things you think are dead. You will not wrinkle your nose at the chaotic parts of your life.

Instead you will be ready for surprise. And I will always be ready to smile at the look on your face when it happens!

Prayer

Surprise me!

Giving

Luke 21:1–4

Jesus looked up and saw rich people putting their gifts into the treasury; he also saw a poor widow put in two small copper coins. He said, 'Truly I tell you, this poor widow has put in more than all of them; for all of them have contributed out of their abundance, but she out of her poverty has put in all she had to live on.'

OUT OF HER POVERTY

All the living she had

The Pilgrim

How hard it is to give out of my poverty. Even in times of abundance it is not always easy to give myself to another. I have to trust. Even then, I have other friends to fall back on. I could always take the risk because at worst I might be disappointed.

But now, in poor times, in the poverty of this illness, to trust is to trust my whole life. I am in the hands of my friends and family and doctors. I am in the hands of this illness. To give out of my poverty is to risk all. For I have little to start with and everything to hope for.

Ironically, I have less choice now than I had in the abundant times. With the advantages of good health, confidence and freedom, I had much to offer others. It felt good to help them. It felt good to trust my life to you. I took my life for granted. I was happy to put myself into relationships and work. When I prayed, I had the riches of many experiences to choose from. Not so much was at stake. I could give thanks and was glad to ask for help in the occasional difficult time.

But now, in my poverty, I find it difficult to offer my life to you. Now everything is at stake. Life and the quality of life has become very precious. I have discovered this my Lord: the less you have, the more you have to lose. The less you have, the more you have to find. And strangely, the less you have, the more you need to give. I find myself the poor widow in your temple.

I come now to offer you everything I have. The little I have can no longer be divided. It is give all or give nothing. And to give nothing, to hope for nothing, would bring a desolation too terrible to contemplate. Yet, how hard I hang on to the little I have.

Out of my poverty, Lord, I put everything into the treasury of our relationship. I put in all the living I have now—a full two copper coins worth.

The Lord

Your illness is the road less travelled. It is the narrow gate to my kingdom, the way of the poor in spirit. Do not be afraid. Your gift is precious to me. Your life is precious to me. In giving all the living you have, you give me more than you have in the past.

Your life feels limited, but now you realise how precious it is. You feel threatened, but now you see how much is at stake. In abundant times it is easy to take the ordinary gifts for granted. Health, peace of mind and the strength to make your own way—all these gifts are so easily assumed.

Now your desires are honed sharp by your poverty. Now you seek healing in the marrow of your spirit. I treasure your offering. Trust me with all your living, with all your needs and wants. Trust me with the small coins of your hope.

In return I offer you my trust. I will risk my life with yours. I offer you my friendship and healing. In your darkness I will place a light that will never go out—the light of acceptance. With this light you will rejoice in who you are now. In your hunger I will feed you bread that will never run out—the bread of life. With this bread you will live life to the full whatever the circumstances. In your thirst I will bring you water that never ends—the water of trust. With this water you will have a trust that loves without expectation or fear. I will join my spirit to yours.

Ours is the treasure greater than all the gold in the world. It is the treasurie of our God's love. So drink more deeply, eat more heartily and lighten the dark. Spend this treasure well and rejoice in the way your God has chosen for you.

Prayer

I have only two copper coins to give you my Lord. The days of riches in my life have passed. My whole living is small. I can do little and my poverty is great. I offer you my whole life as it is now. Accept my offering.

I have only two copper coins. One for my hunger and one for my hope. Take them both and give me your grace and your love. For if I cannot find life where I am now then my one companion will be darkness.

I have only two copper coins. They are not even one-hundredth of a day's wage. I cannot earn more. I am in the hands of my friends and my illness. But the little I can do each day, I will offer to you.

Give me light, food and water to sustain me. Feel the hungers of my heart, quench the thirst of my spirit, lighten the darkness of my days.

I have only two copper coins to give you, my Lord. You have given me yourself. You have emptied the treasury of your heart. In my poverty I am

rich beyond imagination. Give me the wisdom to
spend well the coin of your love.

Mystery

Luke 23:44–46

It was now about the sixth hour, and darkness came over the whole land until three in the afternoon, while the sun's light failed; and the curtain of the temple was torn in two. Then Jesus, crying with a loud voice, said, 'Father, into your hands I commend my spirit.'

Having said this, he breathed his last.

DARKNESS
I commend my spirit

The Pilgrim

'The problem is . . . Many times I use these
words when I am trying to explain my illness to
others. Often I turn these three words on my
tongue when I am talking to my own heart. Endless inner conversations begin with 'If only . . . '
and end with 'But the problem is . . . ' I even
speak of the symptoms of my illness as problems: the problem of mobility, the problem of
concentration, the problem of feeling down, the
problem of trying new things, of waiting, of
work, of body, mind and spirit.

It seems my life is one big problem that I do
not know how to solve. I keep thinking that if I
could find an answer, or at least understanding,
then everything would be all right and I would
get better.

I keep wrestling with myself. At times I feel
guilty that I am ill. I search my past for the reasons
I became like this. But even with some under-

standing, the past does not help much now. I find myself in the dark territory of suffering. The problem is that I feel powerless to find my way out, or my way through, or my way back to where I was before this illness.

What is it about suffering that slips through the fingers of understanding? To question suffering is to learn that there are no answers—not in the sense of finding control. Suffering is elusive. My mind cannot capture it. Yet it has captured me. I used to think that suffering was jaggered with pain, but it has a smooth shape, smooth as a black night. There are no handles. One must either rest in it, or fight it, knowing there is no way to hold it. And to fight suffering is to fight oneself.

What are the choices, Lord? Fatalism? Uneasy truce? Grin and bear it? Romantic melancholy? Buy a pair of rose-coloured glasses? More anger?

The problem is, my Lord, when all is said and done, I feel lost in the darkness of this suffering.

The Lord

The problem with you is that there is no problem, only mystery. Problems invite solutions and resolutions. They often bring anxiety and pain. Mystery invites silence and acceptance. It can even bring wonder.

When one begins an inner journey, one soon comes face-to-face with mystery. As humans there is a part of ourselves that we will never know. There comes a time when we are rudely brought to confront the mystery of ourselves, and very often it can be the most mundane circumstances that bring us to this place. We know this place precisely when we discover there is no way out, or ahead or through or back. We simply are where you are—powerless and in unknown territory.

This is not a problem. It is, in its own way, a profound grace . . . a gift of being. For in this mystery is not only the mystery of yourself, but the mystery of all creation, of all suffering and of all grace, of darkness and light, of you and me, of you and your God.

For compulsive problem solvers, for strong people, for leaders and doers, for people already carrying other burdens, living with mystery can be a frightening time—an hour of darkness like no other.

I know the feeling. For me the problem was that I would die a failure. I lived my whole life, all my hopes, between the sixth and ninth hour. On the cross I commended my spirit to darkness and mystery. Into the mystery of the Creator's will I breathed my last.

I can only ask you to join me there. Commit your life into our God's hands. Rest in the darkness. Rest in the mystery of yourself. You do not need answers. Answers will take you away from the mystery of your true self.

Rather, open your heart to the mystery of suffering. Open your spirit to the mystery of your God who created you in love and who knows the very depths of your being. In time you will become as children—beings who can play and revel in mystery.

Prayer

Into your hands, my Lord, I commend my spirit. My world is in darkness and I cannot see the way to go. I cannot move. I wrestle with myself and find no release from all my problems.

Before now I appeared to have some control in my life. Now it seems my life is in your hands. The initiative is wholly with you. The problem is that it is also in my hands. Who elese can live my life but me? I am snared in the darkness of mystery.

In the past I have bolted from this place as fast as the nearest distraction would take me. But now, by your grace and in your love, I hear the invitation to stay.

I will try. Give me the courage and the patience to wait in the mystery of my being. Guide me. Surround me. Enliven me. Recreate me. Play in me.

Between the sixth and ninth hour of my life, bring the mystery of myself into the mystery of my Creator's hands.

And in the tenth hour, may I breathe my first breath as you breathed your last—in surrender and in the sure hope of resurrection.

Being

Luke 10:38–42

Now as they went on their way, he entered a certain village, where a woman named Martha welcomed him into her home. She had a sister named Mary, who sat at the Lord's feet and listened to what he was saying.

But Martha was distracted by her many tasks; so she came to him and asked, 'Lord, do you not care that my sister has left me to do all the work by myself? Tell her then to help me.' But the Lord answered her, 'Martha, Martha, you are worried and distracted by many things; there is need of only one thing. Mary has chosen the better part, which will not be taken away from her.'

SIT AND LISTEN

There is need of only one thing

The Pilgrim

I have two friends, Lord, who have travelled with me throughout my illness. One gently nudges me to action, the other sits with me and listens. One is energetic and sometimes pushy. The other is gentle and affirming. One is the voice that dances ahead of me, inviting me out of my small world. The other is the voice beside me, encouraging me to let events take their course.

Both care for me. Both support and challenge me. Both have often changed roles. Each has the other within. Each has shared the other side of themselves. I am rich with such friends.

In my own heart I am struck by the resonance of their voices. There is both the one who wants to act and the one who wants to be, the active and the contemplative. I am more comfortable with acting than with being. Even when I know I have to stop working, I soon find myself filling up the hours with small worries and useless little jobs. Is your spirit teaching me something very important through my friends?

If I am pushing myself and I receive a visit from my energetic friend, I soon find myself in trouble. This voice joins the active voice in me. I push harder and I am soon frustrated.

If I have convinced myself that some boundaries in my life are not going to be crossed for a long time, and I receive a visit from my gentle friend, I soon find myself becoming trapped. This voice joins the contemplative voice in me and I begin to retreat into myself. I begin to drag my feet at any change.

On the other hand, when each friend balances the voice within I am challenged and I grow. Is balance what it is all about my Lord? Is there not a time for both Martha and Mary? What did you mean when you said, 'there is need only of one thing'?

The Lord

How much this illness is teaching you! You are beginning to discern the voices of your heart and this is marvellous. Balance is a good thing. However, the true meaning of 'being' is not to be found by putting it opposite 'doing'.

Being is both action and rest. Listening is action without movement. If you listen to your being before me you will learn something beyond balance. The contemplative voice of your heart knows this intuitively. To listen to your being, you must first invite the active voice of your heart to join you at my feet.

At first this sort of listening will appear to be like climbing an unreachable mountain. The temptation will always be to push yourself, to shape yourself to some new self-image. In this, even the image of yourself as a contemplative or a good listener is a temptation.

The way of your being is to let go and risk whatever happens. Just let yourself 'be' quietly before me. Leave all your expectations to another time. Do not try to mend anything. Being is just another way of saying 'to be oneself'. A small time each day will be enough. It is not work or rest. It is both and it is neither. It is. It is as you are. It is as you are before me.

When you come to hold your being in this way you will feel a great release of energy and life. Then, working or resting, you will be true to your being. You will take this habit of listening to your being into your active life. You will be a contemplative in action.

Every small act will be as if you are sitting at my feet listening to my word. Every experience, every breath of your life will be both a prayer and an unfolding of your true being.

Only one thing is necessary in your life. Sit at the feet of your own heart. You will hear my voice speaking in your being. You will soon discover that you have chosen the better part. It will never be taken away from you.

Prayer

Send me your Spirit when I am restless and do not know whether to act or to rest. Send me good friends who search my heart and know me. Come into my presence Lord. Be welcome in my home.

Give me the grace to rest at your feet. Lead me to the truth of my own being. Give me the courage to rest at the feet of my own heart. May the voices I hear lead me to my innermost self.

It is hard to find even a little time to sit quietly with you. It seems impossible when so many distractions and worries steal my peace. Give me the grace to know when to invite the active voice of my heart to join me at your feet.

Help me to be patient. Help me to avoid acting too early or judging too quickly. Help me not to lose heart too soon. Free me from the habit of owning each experience too quickly and then dismissing it. Teach me the habit of savouring life and my life with others. Teach me the habit of being and being with you. Free me from all expectations in the true unfolding of my being.

May I sit and relish all that is opened to me. May I carry the voice of my full being into every act, every encounter, every breath of my life.

May I become contemplative in action.

Forgiveness
Luke 7:36–50

One of the Pharisees asked Jesus to eat with him, and he went into the Pharisee's house and took his place at the table. And a woman in the city, who was a sinner, having learned that he was eating in the Pharisee's house, brought an alabaster jar of ointment. She stood behind him at his feet, weeping, and began to bathe his feet with her tears and to dry them with her hair. Then she continued kissing his feet and anointing them with the ointment.

Now when the Pharisee who had invited him saw it, he said to himself, 'If this man were a prophet, he would have known who and what kind of woman this is who is touching him— that she is a sinner.'

Jesus spoke up and said to him, 'Simon, I have something to say to you.' 'Teacher,' he replied, 'Speak.' 'A certain creditor had two debtors; one owed five hundred denarii, and the other fifty. When they could not pay, he cancelled the debts for both of them. Now which of them will love him more?' Simon answered, 'I suppose the one for whom he cancelled the greater debt.'

And Jesus said to him, 'You have judged rightly.' Then turning toward the woman, he said to Simon, 'Do you see this woman? I entered your house; you gave me no water for my feet, but she has bathed my feet with her tears and dried them with her hair. You gave me no kiss, but from the time I came in she has not stopped kissing my feet. You did not anoint my head with oil, but she has anointed my feet with ointment.

'Therefore, I tell you, her sins, which were many, have been forgiven; hence she has shown great love. But the one to whom little is forgiven, loves little.' Then he said to her, 'Your sins are forgiven.'

But those who were at the table with him began to say among themselves, 'Who is this who even forgives sins?'

And he said to the woman, 'Your faith has saved you; go in peace.'

SHE IS A SINNER

She has shown great love

The Pilgrim

Lord, I am deeply unsettled. The feeling of help-lessness is assuming a life of its own. It has grown strong. It has entered unannounced into our time together. I can no longer ignore it. I have begun to hate it.

Many times I have felt angry and fed up with my illness. My feelings seemed natural enough, but lately I have begun to hate my illness. I have begun to feel disgusted with myself when I am helpless and ill. Underneath the anger and fear I have found self-hatred.

Now there is a conflict within me. The feeling of helplessness is growing into a deep desire for self-forgiveness—a desire for support and accep-tance of the helpless self. This desire wants room in my heart to love and be loved. But the more this desire grows, the more I find myself rejecting it.

In my prayer, I like to have things just right.

You are no ordinary guest. I like to have my house in order, to set a worthy meal before you. I like to feel you are welcome and enjoy my company. And when I pray for healing, I like to feel positive. I like to count the good things in my life and invite the good experiences, such as friends, to our table. But now I am embarrassed.

Two new faces have intruded into my life: the desire for forgiveness and the hatred of that desire. I never knew I could feel self-hatred. It has never been a part of my living, or at least not a part that I have ever been aware of before. I have tried to keep both faces away from our meetings, but it is useless. They are here and all my plans for a nice relationship have been spoiled.

What is this desire for forgiveness and love, Lord? How was it born from my feeling of helplessness? Why did it grow so strong in the living of my illness? Why did it make such a noisy entrance into my life? Why do I feel both gladdened and alarmed? What is this desire, and why do I hate it so much?

The Lord

You know what this desire is. It is the desire that springs from your sinfulness. It was born in the place where you are powerless to change yourself. It grew strong in the helpless part of your life. It is that part of your illness you hate in yourself, and there are times when you loathe it.

You feel alarmed because this feeling of helplessness is the one thing you cannot share with your closest friends, or even with yourself. It is that part of yourself rarely seen—so it made a noisy entrance.

Until you welcome this feeling you will be fighting a losing battle with yourself. It will weigh on you every time you cannot forgive yourself, or ask for forgiveness. It will be there every time you make plans that do not include the possibility of your own sinfulness. It is, and always has been, a part of your humanity. It is where you are unfree. Your illness has simply revealed what was always there. It will be with you to the last day of your life.

You know this feeling well. You know this deep desire for wholeness and forgiveness. So you feel gladdened. Until now you had not come face-to-face with it. You had not experienced the deeper need that is rooted in your helplessness. That is why I welcome this desire in you.

You always work hard to make everything right for me. You like to bring the good things in your life to me. This is good. But this new feeling has brought your sinfulness, your tears and your desire to love me even as a sinner. This is even better. It is a cause for great joy.

A part of you still hates all this. It wishes to avoid embarrassment, to deny the need for forgiveness and healing. But there is a great gift being offered here, and it is much more important than pride.

Let this new desire for forgiveness stay with us. Rejoice that it feels free to come into my presence. Let go your hatred. Through your great love, the love that acknowledges sinfulness before me, I have already forgiven you. Forgive yourself. Forgive the feeling of helplessness.

Learn to love your enemy. Love your enemy like yourself.

Prayer

You know me through and through my Lord. I thought I could invite you to my table and you would see only what I wanted you to see.

I could not invite the part of my illness that I hate in myself. I could not welcome the unsettling face of sinfulness to our table. I did not think that this was a part of me that you would care to meet. What revolted me, I thought would revolt you. What I hate in myself, I thought you would hate. And then I thought you would hate me.

But you do not. You see my whole heart and a heart divided. How can I love this part of myself as you do? How can I forgive myself as you do?

My illness has uncovered an intolerance that I never knew about. Yet I think it was always there. I have always disliked the chaos in myself. Yet now I see how much that part of myself wants to meet you. A deeply shamed self desires to be a part of my love for you. Please forgive me.

When I am hard on myself, when I feel self-hatred, let me understand the idols in my heart that provoke such a feeling—the idols of the ideal me and the ideal you.

Let me seek your presence without all the preparations. May I come as I am. Help me to forgive myself. Give me the grace and the love to bring all of myself to the table with you.

Liberation

Luke 24:33–48

That same hour the two disciples got up and
returned to Jerusalem; and they found the
eleven and their companions gathered together.
They were saying, 'The Lord has risen indeed,
and he has appeared to Simon!' Then they
told what had happened on the road, and
how he had been made known to them in the
breaking of the bread.

While they were talking about this, Jesus himself stood among them and said to them, 'Peace
be with you.' They were startled and terrified,
and thought that they were seeing a ghost.

He said to them, 'Why are you frightened,
and why do doubts arise in your hearts? Look
at my hands and my feet; see that it is I myself. Touch me and see; for a ghost does not
have flesh and bones as you see that I have.'
And when he had said this, he showed them
his hands and his feet. While in their joy they
were disbelieving and still wondering, he said
to them, 'Have you anything here to eat?'
They gave him a piece of broiled fish, and he
took it and ate in their presence.

Then he said to them, 'These are my words that I spoke to you while I was still with you—that everything written about me in the law of Moses, the prophets, and the psalms must be fulfilled.'

Then he opened their minds to understand the scriptures, and he said to them, 'Thus it is written, that the Messiah is to suffer and to rise from the dead on the third day, and that repentance and forgiveness of sins is to be proclaimed in his name to all nations, beginning from Jerusalem.

'You are witnesses of these things.'

TOUCH ME AND SEE

You are witnesses of these things

The Pilgrim

The door is closed and locked. Four strong walls
surround me. My inner self is safe. Here I can
survive. I need these walls. My illness raised
them and my old fears bolted the door. This is
the last sanctuary.

I need this refuge, this room of last resort.
How else can I be healed? How else can I rest
and let the world go by? These walls protect me.
Outside so few understand this disease. They
have never had to live a life around a body of
few resources. Yet I am not bitter. I am sure I
will get over the lost hopes. In fact I am resolved
about the future. You have healed me in many
ways, Lord, and I can live with my life as it is. I
still need this room but few will notice.

Anyone who has suffered over a long time
knows the walls I have built. It was not a quick
building. The walls were raised slowly. Each
stone was found in each experience of frustra-

tion and pain, of loss and survival. This strong-room in my heart is not a good thing or a bad thing. It just is. Given my experiences, it was inevitable.

The walls of this room were raised over the years. At first it was just a foxhole to run to when times were bad. Then it was a breakwater to shelter from the storms of my illness. So gradually it built up: a wall, another stone, another wall, a tower, a fastness, an upper room with a stout door.

And now, be it haven or prison, it is where I keep my inner self. Be it grim avoidance or stark reality, it is now a part of my life. God knows what others do.

I believe that even if there were comfort outside I would not leave this room to receive it. The scars run too deep and I would protect the little I have left. I may not be at peace, but I am resolved. It is enough for survival. And if the help outside was insistent, I could not unbolt the door and they could not break through.

The very pattern of my life now defies hope. Such is the stamp this illness has left on my body and spirit.

The Lord

Peace be with you. Your walls cannot hold me out. Even suffering and death cannot hold me out . . . and I bring the suffering with me. See my hands and my feet. See the scars. Touch them and see. I do understand. It was the Creator's will to resurrect me precisely so I could stand in this place with you.

Touch my wounds to yours! Feel my Father's love. Flesh to my flesh—touch and see. I am not a figment of your imagination. I have come here through the walls of disappointment and help-lessness. I have walked through the stones of suffering and fear. The stones of sorrow and pride cannot block me. I have come to liberate you.

Let the unbeliever in you put his hand into the wound in my side. I am really here. Let the scep-tic in you eat broiled fish with me. Ghosts do not eat. Let the fearful one in you see that the door is still bolted. Yet I am here.

Touch me. Feel the healed wounds. Trace the

pattern of my life in my hands. Trace the pattern of your life in my hands. So it was written that I should suffer and on the third day rise from the dead. This is the pattern of my life. This is the pattern of your life.

I have come here to liberate you. There is more to your life than survival. In coming through these walls I have shown you a way out. I have come to heal your wounds in this place of last resort. Here my spirit binds with yours and hope is not lost. It rests on God's love.

You are a witness to all these things and these things need to be proclaimed in my name to all nations—beginning from this room!

Prayer

You startled the life out of me when you walked through the wall. I did not know what to say. I thought those walls were unbreakable facts of life.

Yet you walked through my suffering and self-protection. You passed through the stones of my illness and stand here offering companionship and hope.

My Lord, you healed me when you showed me your wounds. You liberated me when you showed me that the pattern of your life could be mine. It is mine, and now I see it will be mine again and again. In all my dying will be the seeds of rising.

There is still much I do not understand. My will is still beggared by my fear. My life is still compassed by my illness. I still have my memories. I still need your healing. Yet I feel the beginnings of liberation. You have freed me within the fastness of my being, the stronghold of my heart.

Now you are my refuge. Now I am surrounded by the walls of your love. You are my fortress, a mighty stronghold to save me. Give me the grace to be a witness to all these things. Give me the grace to pray the prayer of your son, St Ignatius:

Take, Lord, and receive all my liberty,
my memory, my intellect, and all my will—
all that I have and possess.
You gave it to me.
To you, Lord, I return it.
All is yours, dispose of it according to your will.
Give me only Your love and grace,
for this is enough for me.

Ordinariness
Luke 17:20-21

Once Jesus was asked by the Pharisees when the kingdom of God was coming, and he answered, 'The kingdom of God is not coming with things that can be observed; nor will they say, "Look, here it is!" or "There it is!" For, in fact, the kingdom of God is among you.'

THE KINGDOM OF GOD
It is among you

The Pilgrim

Now that the weather of my spirit has calmed I am beginning to realise what I have really missed in my life—the joy of the ordinary, the satisfaction of small goals and the company of everyday experiences. It makes a welcome change from the hurricanes of my illness, from the black thunder-heads of my feelings, from the flash floods of my heart.

So often in my illness things have become larger than life. Feelings swing high and low, dreams arrive in primal technicolour, and peace is but a small child held between the adults of crisis.

In the storms that flash and crack through my being I search for meaning. In suffering relapse I endlessly probe for solutions.

It is all high drama! But what is the plot? I strain to understand as the characters of my illness dance and caper on the stage. Black-clad characters deliver fearful monologues, emotions parade like a troupe of contortionists—stretching and pulling disappointment to anger, bending and folding hopes to grief. Memories hold the stage like vaudeville comedians. My life is grand opera and farce, Greek tragedy and circus folly! And just when I think I understand, the stage-hands rush in and change all the props.

Lord, someone has thrown the script of my life out of the window. How I wished I could point with sudden insight and say 'There! There is the meaning of my life.' How often I have longed to cry 'Look! Here it is. Here is the meaning of my suffering.' But I was never able to do this. Now I tire of the effort.

Thank God for the change! Now the show is over, Lord, and I feel your presence in the sawdust of the empty ring. Now the house lights are back on, and I discover you sitting beside me. Lord of my life, Lord of the calm after the storm, Lord of the empty stage, Lord of the ordinary, it is good to see you here.

The Lord

You remind me of the years I spent working as a carpenter for my father. I loved the feel of well-worked wood, the pleasure in making ordinary chairs and tables, and the smell of varnish and wood shavings. You remind me of the days on the road during my ministry. I cherished the company of good friends, simple meals and laughter at night under the stars.

There were those who never understood. They looked for signs and wonders. They plied me with questions, but I was never the Messiah they were looking for. They looked for the kingdom of God. They were blind. I saw it all around me.

I saw it in the planting and harvesting of wheat, in the sheep led to pasture and in the visit to Simon's mother. I saw it in the breaking of bread, in the drawing of water at the village well and in the lighting of the lamp. I saw it in the shame of the tax collector, in the hands of a fisherman, in the eyes of a prostitute, in the offering of a widow, in the death of a thief and in the curiosity of children. It was right under our noses.

I found it in the well-built house, in the tower and the arch, in the fish and the stone and the wineskin, in the yeast and the sparrow. I discovered it in the soldier and the bridegroom, in the virgin and the adulterer, in the steward and the farmer's son. It showed itself in the cry of daybreak, in the freeing of a debt, in the wine of a wedding feast and in breakfast on the beach. In the ordinary lives of ordinary people, I found the kingdom of God.

Oh, it was present too in the storm and the flood, in the slaughter of innocents, in the betrayal and in the whip and the cross. It shouted in the silence of the deaf and in the babble of the possessed. It whispered in the cry of the beggar. It was there too in the darkness and the drama. But for the listening and the understanding, for the change of heart and just action, and for the love deeply rooted, you need the time of the ordinary.

Then your eyes and ears, your hands and your heart will be opened. You will discover that the kingdom of God is among you.

Prayer

God of the ordinary, walk with me now. Help me to see your kingdom in the little things, in the everyday world of my dressing-gown pocket.

May your love twine into the light chatter of friends, into my favourite morning tea biscuit, the shade of a tree, the washing, the ironing, and into all the things of no great moment that fill my day.

As for the drama of my illness—I say let the stars fall from the skies! Forget the grand designs, the signs and portents. Good riddance to all the ultimate meanings, the make-up and sound effects. Give me rather your presence in the ordinary events of my life.

So when the confusions of my illness enlarge to fill the horizon of my day, give me the patience to wait without anxiety. When the feelings stretch out of shape, and relapse rewrites the script, give me the confidence not to search for great meaning. Give me the courage to remember gentler times.

And if my inner life must turn to high drama, give me the faith to sit back with you and enjoy the show. For when these times are over, I know you will be at my side, waiting for the house lights to come on and a companionable walk home.

Feasting
Luke 14:12-14

Jesus said also to the one who had invited him, 'When you give a feast or a dinner, do not invite your friends or your brothers or your relatives or rich neighbours, in case they may invite you in return, and you would be repaid. But when you give a banquet, invite the poor, the crippled, the lame, and the blind. And you will be blessed, because they cannot repay you, for you will be repaid at the resurrection of the righteous.'

GIVE A BANQUET
Invite the poor and the crippled

The Pilgrim

A lot has happened over the last five years, my
Lord. It has been a real feast of illness. I have
shared it with friends and family. Now with signs
of recovery I sense that my friends are waiting
for me to return to 'normal'. But I will not be the
same as before. This illness has changed me.

A long illness shrinks one's world. In the
struggle to cope I found that my well-being
became the focus of my awareness. It is said that
suffering creates character. It is written that
patience leads to hope and grace. This is true,
but there is another side. What is never said is
that suffering strips away many of the good
qualities. Darker characters are brought to the
surface. I found I was crankier, more impatient,
more selfish, judgemental, harder on myself and
others. I became blind to the small needs of others
around me. I needed the realistic perspective of
friends to read my choices about lifestyle. And I

did not always welcome them. If there is a grace in all this it is that I am more aware of my short-comings.

In the past I could share out my life and myself in comfortable parcels. I cannot do this now. Having experienced my own fragility, I must find life in all of myself—the strong and the weak. Only this way can I live at peace with myself.

My Lord, I am a little apprehensive about this new awareness. Yet I have a sense of oneness with others who have suffered. I feel less in control, but more at home in the world. After the feast of living with chronic illness I would dine again with others outside my small world.

I would dine with you, my Lord, at your table with the poor, the crippled, the blind and the lame.

The Lord

I have earnestly desired to eat this meal with you. Take the cup of my suffering and drink. Share it with others. Take the bread of my body. Break it open. Share it with others.

Take the cup of your own suffering. Drink and share it with others. Take the bread of your own body. You have been broken open. Your life is a banquet, a feast to be shared. I bless all of your life and give thanks.

You have discovered the undeniable reality of our humanity—its fragility, sinfulness and neediness. You have been graced with new strengths. You cannot return to blind ignorance. Although you may hobble all your life, you will not be alone.

I have longed to eat this meal with you. Invite the blind and the lame, the poor and the crippled. They too starve for life. They too desire healing in their inner selves. They too hunger for truth and justice. Like you they are searching. Like you they are pilgrims—ever restless, ever wanting, ever longing for company and the chance to rejoice on the way.

I never intended our relationship to be only personal. I came for the whole community of humanity. You know that suffering and illness are great levellers. So is love. I came to break all distinctions: rich and poor, black and white, loved or unloved, broken or whole, wise or foolish. The feast of my resurrection breaks the power of darkness and slavery. It calls for the creation of a just and loving community.

I call you my friend and disciple. I invite you to go out beyond the circle of your family and friends. I invite you to celebrate the eucharist of our lives. I invite you to break the simple bread of your humanity with the hungry.

Prayer

Lord, help me to see beyond the small world of my illness. With the insight my illness has brought me, give me the outsight to see the lame and the poor and the crippled. And seeing them, give me the courage to break open my life with them.

My Lord, I too have been poor and lame. My illness has maimed me for good. And for 'good' my life is filled with riches. Let all my disabilities be signs of your healing and your gospel.

Call me out Lord. Call me out of my self, out of my self-pity, out of my darkness, out of my blindness, out of my small dreams. Call me Lord. Call me to those who suffer injustice, to those who suffer poverty, to those who live in darkness. Call me to the light that shows the world as it is. Call me to large dreams. Call me with those who share my faith, and with those who do not.

Feed me Lord. Feed me with your body and spirit. Show me how to share my life in the community where I live.

Heal me in the breaking of your body, in the heart of your love, in the gathering of your people, in the feast of our lives.

EPILOGUE

Blessed be the God and Father of our Lord Jesus Christ, the Father of mercies and the God of all consolation, who consoles us in all our affliction, so that we may be able to console those who are in any affliction with the consolation with which we ourselves are consoled by God.

2 Corinthians 1:3–4

REFERENCES

Mark 8:22–25 Introduction
Ephesians 3:14–21 Prologue
Luke 1:36–37 Barrenness
Luke 2:1–12 Poverty
Luke 5:17–26 Paralysis
Luke 4:1–13 Power
Luke 4:16–30 Anger
Luke 7:11–15 Grief
Luke 8:43–48 Illness
Luke 7:1–10 Words
Luke 6:47–49 Relapse
Luke 8:26–33, 38–39 Chains
Luke 12:22–31 Anxiety
Luke 5:1–11 Despair

Luke 23:33–46 Panic
Luke 8:40–42, 49–55 Death
Luke 5:12–13 Time
Luke 11:5–13 Prayer
Luke 15:11–24 Compassion
Luke 24:1–12 Surprise
Luke 21:1–4 Giving
Luke 23:44–46 Mystery
Luke 10:38–42 Being
Luke 7:36–50 Forgiveness
Luke 24:33–48 Liberation
Luke 17:20–21 Ordinariness
Luke 14:12–14 Feasting
Corinthians 1:1–4 Epilogue